Christianity and the Class Struggle

Christianity and the Class Struggle

HAROLD O. J. BROWN

Introductory note by
BILLY GRAHAM

ZONDERVAN PUBLISHING HOUSE
GRAND RAPIDS, MICHIGAN

Contents

Introductory Note

In these pages Harold O. J. Brown comes to grips with some of the gigantic problems that face the world and Christendom. He deals with them forthrightly and "without gloves." He dares to attack some of the materialistic greats and some of the fallacies they advocated, which have since been discredited. While one may disagree with Dr. Brown here and there, the main body of this work is challenging to the mind and refreshing to the spirit. He looks realistically at the race question. He laments the tendency of professed Christian leaders to scoff at their only textbook, the Bible, and to cherish unquestioningly the theories of materialistic and secularistic philosophy. He calls for reformation instead of revolution, and says that a system that puts class against class is of the devil. Words could not be clearer in his denunciation of heresy, and in his demand for a return to a New Testament faith.

—Dr. Billy Graham
Montreat, North Carolina

Foreword

"If the trumpet give an uncertain sound," asks St. Paul, "who shall prepare himself to the battle?" (1 CORINTHIANS 14:8). The churches which profess allegiance to Jesus Christ, despite the inroads of secularism and persecution, nevertheless still represent a formidable segment of the world's population. If even ten percent of the world's professing Christians were systematically to *act* as Christians in even one area of their lives—in speech, in social responsibility, in questions of personal morality—a great many things would change around the world. But so much of official Christendom and of Christian officialdom gives forth uncertain sounds that very few prepare themselves for the battle. And we are in a battle today, one with many fronts and many levels: spiritual, moral, intellectual, political, to mention but a few. In the chapters that follow, I deal with a subject that I believe to be of central importance to the Christian and to the world. I have tried to do it in a simple way, and I am sure that many will find it too simple. But I am deeply convinced that there is no place for the trumpet that gives an uncertain sound among the followers of Christ in our day.

Lausanne, Switzerland
July 14, 1970

Foreword TO ZONDERVAN EDITION

Over two years have passed since the major part of this book was written, and in that time, many things have happened. I am grateful to the editors of the Zondervan Publishing House for permitting me to add certain corrections and the revisions which appeared most necessary. The thesis, of course, remains unchanged, and I believe—whether it is well or badly expressed here—that it is of vital importance for the future of God's people in this world, as well as for mankind as a whole. No racial wars have broken out yet—if we make exception of the totally unexpected carnage which has taken place in East Pengal. The racial situation in the United States seems quieter than one might have expected, and yet bloody incidents like those at San Quentin and Attica prisons, as well as continuing resentment on all sides over the school busing issue, show that there may be much worse still to come. At the same time, our good evangelical churches, both in the South as well as in the North, seem for the most part to be dreaming away the God-given months or years of deceptive calm, instead of building strong, personal, Christian ties between the races while there is yet time. May God enable us to escape our dreaming lethargy, but not, as it were, to plunge down the slope into the sea with the swine, but to take distinctive action worthy of witnesses of Jesus Christ.

Deerfield, Illinois
October 14, 1971

1.

The Specter and the Struggle

THE specter that stalked Europe, in the words of the *Communist Manifesto*, has taken on flesh and blood. It dominates one third of the human beings on this planet, and would gladly, we may be sure, extend its domination to the remaining two thirds. To all those who cherish political, economic, religious, and intellectual liberty, the physical reality of communism is no idle threat. Most Christians, with good cause, used to look upon communism as a paramount danger to the existence of Christianity and to the humanity of man. Church leaders, from the late Pope Pius XII down to many local pastors and priests, once felt that it was their calling to marshal the forces of Christendom against it. Now all this has changed. We are in the age of "dialogue with the Marxists." Sometimes the Christians participating in such "dialogue" appear realistic and hard-headed; sometimes they seem to be gullible fools, but whatever they may be, dialogue is in, Christian anti-communist crusades are not. Not everyone will agree with the author of *Tortured for Christ*, the exiled Rumanian Lutheran pastor Richard Wurmbrand, in feeling that many ecumenical and denominational bodies as well as most Christians in the West are playing into the hands of scheming Communists and thereby betraying suffering witnesses in Communist-dominated areas. It is hard to deny, though, that instead of the militant hard line on "godless Communism," many church leaders and organizations now seem to have taken the motto of the three monkeys of Lausanne: See no evil, hear no evil, speak no evil.

Forty miles from Lausanne, in the corridors of the Ecumenical Church Center at Geneva, W.C.C. leaders will admit in private conversations that the continuing Communist pressure on Christians is no secret for them. But they have decided to try the path of dialogue, and now they must preserve a discreet silence about everything which might irritate their dialogue partners or merit the disapproval of the Communist authorities on whom the continuation of the dialogue depends.[1]

Concerning our ecumenical leaders and others active in such dialogue, we would like to feel that although their mouths are sealed, their eyes are not. Our eyes, in any event, are still open. We are perfectly clear about the fact that Communism, both the international and the domestic variety, does constitute a real threat to Christianity, just as it does to the measure of political and economic freedom which is to be found in the Western or "bourgeois' democracies. Some hopeful or naive souls now argue that Russian communism has abandoned its politics of aggression and suppression and that the Church need no longer suspect it; even the Russian invasion of Czechoslovakia in August 1968 seems to have dampened these hopes only slightly. The idea is that Russian communism is becoming "mellow," civilized, peaceful, almost middle-class, and that real aggression needs to be feared at most on the part of

[1] Certainly this feeling had something to do with the abandonment by the N.C.C. of support for Dr. Blahoslav Hruby's excellent and unique documentation of Christian life in Communist countries, the periodical known as *Religion in Communist Dominated Lands*.

the Chinese and their adherents. Now, of course—especially since President Nixon's dramatic new China policy—it is no longer fashionable to suspect even the Chinese Communists and their adherents of being anything other than men of good will. It is an unfortunate feature of the American mind that we seem unable to imagine that any people or group could be motivated over a long period by any goals more serious or more firmly held than our own.

It is not our purpose here to contend that the Communist powers have not mellowed. It seems clear enough that they still constitute a formidable threat to the peace of the world and to the freedom of those nations where communism is not yet established. Rather, our task is to consider a different threat, one which comes from within the "free" societies themselves. This threat may be, and undoubtedly is, being promoted and encouraged from the outside, by the Soviet Union and Communist China, but it does not originate with them, nor are they themselves immune to it. It is the specter of class struggle. The concept of class struggle was formulated by Marx and Engels, and it has served the purposes of communism well, but class struggle as such did not begin with them in the nineteenth century. It is not likely to end in the twentieth, even in those countries in which communism has triumphed. We are saying, in other words, that our task here is to deal with a problem which goes much deeper than the mere physical threat of Communist military aggression, or of the so-called Communist conspiracy, with a problem, then, which also may become a serious one for the "Communist conspirators."

Because this is our purpose, it is necessary to say that the "simpler" and "smaller" problem, i.e., the *military* and *conspiratorial* threat posed by communism to the non-Communist world, is by no means to be disregarded. It simply is not our subject here. Communism is a military and political entity which has taken up the slogan and the philosophy of the class struggle, and as a very powerful military and political entity it deserves close attention from all those who value their freedom. But communism is not the only way in which the class struggle can manifest itself, and perhaps it is not even the most important for us today. Therefore we shall devote ourselves here not to the specific phenomenon of communism and its present military and political might, but to the larger problem of the class struggle as a political rationale and as a present reality.

The central political reality in the world today is that of class struggle. It takes many forms: the struggle between economic classes, the struggle between races, the struggle between age groups, even the struggle between mentalities, "bourgeois," and "revolutionary." Struggle is familiar to human history, and class struggle on a widespread basis has been known before. But at no time in human history has it been more widespread or blinder than at our own particular historical moment.

What is the central spiritual reality in the world today? Can we claim, either as "cultural" or as actively committed Christians, that *Christianity* is that central spiritual reality? We certainly cannot plausibly maintain that it is the most impressive spiritual or religious *phenomenon* of our day; that is, that it is the most obvious and striking thing to be seen and heard. Perhaps the contentless mysticism of the "new theology" is more of a *phenomenon* than any manifestation of traditional Christianity, which hardly attracts widespread attention or interest.

When we speak of a spiritual *reality*, as opposed to a mere *phenomenon*, however, the situation becomes different. That which is apparent to the senses as a widely observable phenomenon is not necessarily real. (The sunset is a phenomenon that is observed by countless millions every day, and yet in reality the sun never does set.) To inquire about a spiritual *reality* at once takes one out of the area of detached, "objective" discussion of phenomena and plunges him into the question of religious commitment. To observe a particular religious phenomenon is one thing; to claim that a particular religious teaching is true is another. Christianity is a weak *phenomenon* in the world today; its weakness as a phenomenon depends on the number of people who accept it and act accordingly. It can be contended that it is *the central spiritual reality*, however, for that contention depends not on how many people accept it but on whether God established it, that is, on whether it is true. Only the committed Christian will accept Christianity as the central spiritual reality, but any man who can think clearly ought to be able to see that if it is true, then it is central. To see this does not require commitment to the implications of Christian teaching; it requires only an ability to see what those implications are. One great failure on the part of Christians today is their persistent reluctance to take the implications of their own faith seriously. Often they think that thereby they make dialogue with non-Christians possible. In fact, however, they make such dialogue less interesting and less worthwhile.

Here it is necessary to see clearly. The fact that the believing Christian has a commitment of faith which he cannot *prove* scientifically does not disqualify him from speaking out on issues which also affect those who do not share his belief. In fact, it obliges him to do so. It certainly does not oblige him to hide his commitment and to speak "for the sake of argument," as though he were not a Christian. To be a Christian means to accept a certain view of reality, and to accept it as true not merely "for Christians," or "in a religious way," but for all men everywhere and in every age. Many Christians have much to learn about tact and tolerance in witnessing to the "absolutist" claims of their faith. But unless they are willing to face up to their absolute nature, that is, to the fact that if true, they apply to others as well as to Christians, to "politics" as well as to "religion," then they have not understood or accepted the fundamental claim of the Christian message to be true—not merely "beautiful" or "uplifting." Dialogue with such a "Christian" is pointless.

If the basic content of the Christian message is true, then it *is* the central spiritual reality, regardless of what may be the prevalent religious phenomena. It was the central spiritual reality of the world in the months following Christ's death and resurrection, when only a few Jewish and Gentile converts had even heard of it; it was, it did not *become*, the central spiritual reality in the so-called Age of Faith, when all of Europe formally accepted it; it still is the central spiritual reality today, regardless of how secularized society and civilization may become or may already be. All this holds *if* the content is true.

If Earth is, in J. B. Phillips' words, "the visited planet," if, as St. John tells us, "the Word became flesh, and dwelt among us" (JOHN 1:14), then the central spiritual reality is that God has a will, a plan and a goal, if you prefer, for men. The goal is that they become His children (JOHN 1:12).[2] If this central assertion is true, then we dare not

---

[2] Because expressions such as "we are all God's children" are bandied about, it is worth emphasizing that "Jesus did not, of course, teach the liberal Protestant notion that God is Father of all men *qua* men . . . ; God is Father only of those who have by faith and repentance entered into his reign and accepted the obedience of sons." Alan Richardson, *An Introduction to the Theology of the New Testament* (London: S.C.M. Press, 1958), p. 149.

consider any political reality, that is, any expression of human willing and striving, apart from the great spiritual reality which is the will of God for human individuals and for mankind. Perhaps the deepest and most serious weakness in the Christian churches today, and the source of their inability to deal effectively with the modern world, does not lie in the lack of real commitment or genuine faith on the part of so many nominal Christians, as is so often charged. Perhaps it lies in the fact that so many who really do believe that Christianity is true do not know what it means to say that God has visited this planet and has expressed *His* opinion on certain matters. They do not even suspect that God has a will and a plan which must be applied across the board, to the whole range of human problems and not merely to "religious" ones.

The teaching of the Bible does not embrace only "religious" matters. If the revelation of God in Christ really is *true*, then the Christian has to try to obey his Lord not merely in the *religious* sphere, but in the whole of life. This is a truth which is repeated by millions daily in that beloved prayer, "Thy will be done, *on earth as it is in heaven*." To pray this and to take it seriously mean that Christian faith has something to say to the other realities of the world. No one who says the Lord's Prayer should be ignorant of its plain implication that the Father in heaven has a will which is to be fulfilled on earth. In the case at hand, this means that if Christianity applies at all, it also applies, in the case at hand, to the class struggle.

Christian churches and individual Christians have often been accused of otherworldliness. They have been charged with neglecting this world and the practical needs of human beings in order to secure the welfare of their own souls. Being "heavenly minded," they are said to be no earthly good. This charge is not without foundation. Even in New Testament times, St. James had to warn some such heavenly minded disciples against a merely "spiritual" response to man's problems: "If a brother or sister is ill-clad and in lack of daily food, and one of you says to them, 'Go in peace, be warmed and filled,' without giving them the things needed for the body, what does it profit?" (JAMES 2:15–16). But James *did* warn them, and this is part of the New Testament itself, not in criticism of the New Testament.

If Christians are to do justice to the teachings of the New Testament, they must deal with the real problems facing the world, that is, with its political, social, and economic problems. They must thus face every political reality, and paramount among them, the class struggle as the outstanding political reality of our day.

When certain Christian leaders suggest that we should "follow the world's agenda" (*agenda,* Latin, means "things to be done"), they are reacting against the kind of Christianity which has contented itself with "soul-saving" and personal piety without any regard for the physical needs of living, breathing human beings. Such "Christianity," without a heart for man's physical needs, to the extent that it actually exists, is not New Testament Christianity. It should be reacted against—even as James did in his epistle —but the reaction must not be to ignore the truth of the Christian message. Political realities have to be considered in the light of spiritual realities, *not substituted for them.*

To "follow the world's agenda," to do first and foremost what the world would have him do, is not an answer which the Christian can accept. If there is anything to the Christian message, if this is "the visited planet," if God has made Himself and His will known to men in Christ, then we must follow *His* agenda, and do *His* "things to be done." We must not deny or attempt to ignore the political reality: in the case at hand, we must not ignore the class struggle. But we may not allow it to take precedence over

God's agenda. By so doing, we would cease to be true Christians, no matter how much we might protest that we were "making Christianity relevant," or becoming "the church in the world." And in fact God's agenda requires us to deal with the world's problems, but on *His* terms.

If the class struggle is so central to political life, then the Christian is involved in it. His duty as a Christian does not permit him, unless he has a special divine vocation, to withdraw from the life of his fellow human beings: he must remain in their midst. Thus he is automatically in political life, and in the class struggle. The important thing is this: he must remain in their midst *as a committed Christian*, following God's agenda, not casting about to see what comes first in the world's scale of priorities.

The task of the Christian, then, is to bring spiritual reality and political reality into contact. This means specifically that he must look at the class struggle in the light of the reality of Christ, of His teaching, and of His purpose. One may, if one so wishes, ignore the reality of Christ and look only at the class struggle, as a phenomenon on the merely human level. There are many, including prominent churchmen, who do this. If we do so, however, we must admit that we do not in fact take the claims of Christ seriously. Either we do not believe that this planet has been visited by God, in which case we are not Christians at all, or else we think that the pressure of the present historical situation dispenses us from following His agenda. Any allegedly Christian attempt to be responsible in the world is either irresponsible or falsely calls itself Christian if it fails to bring the sovereignty of Christ, which is *the* central spiritual reality, to play upon the political reality.

The Christian is a citizen by nature of this world, with its obligations, and a citizen by grace of the Kingdom of

God. *He* is the link, in his person, between his fellow human beings, who as unbelievers are ignorant of or indifferent to the grace of God, and God's Kingdom. He is like a man on a mountainside holding a rock with one hand and a climber who is about to slip over the edge with the other. To let go of the rock would be to be pulled over himself; to let go of the other man would be to abandon him to destruction. He must hold fast to both until help comes. It is thus as a living bridge between two kingdoms that the Christian must hold to both, neither abandoning the non-Christian world to take refuge in otherworldly piety, nor abandoning God for the world which does not yet acknowledge Him. The radical theologians are right when they say that the churches must go into the world, even (or *especially*) into the class struggle, but they are wrong when they say that this world's criteria must determine the churches' action. The church is in the world as God's expeditionary force. It is to be in the class struggle, but not for the poor against the rich (or vice versa) or for any class against another, but for the love of God against the selfishness and suffering of men.

Class struggle must be considered from two perspectives. First, it is a phenomenon, something which happens in human life when certain conditions prevail. Second, it is a principle. Just as Clausewitz said, "War is politics carried on by other means," so the class struggle has its devotees who say, "The class struggle is progress carried on by other means." For Hitler, struggle and war were not merely legitimate means but the necessary and ideal means to personal and racial self-improvement. He felt that the German race would (to use Ernst Jünger's expression) emerge from "the tempests of steel" purified, strengthened, and ennobled. Advocates of the class struggle as a principle, including not only doctrinaire Marxists, but even people as diverse as the Black Power group and the so-called Living Theatre and its initiators, think that out of a bloodbath which would destroy the current "oppressors" a new, pure mankind, free of greed and vice, will emerge. The philosophy of class struggle is the "civilian equivalent" of the militarists' glorification of war, and it has similar underlying presuppositions.

At a later point we shall consider the philosophical and theological presuppositions which underlie the hope that destroying the present perpetrators of injustice in class struggle (or war) will make the survivors just. For the moment, let us merely note that so far it has never happened. Consider the observation of one of the world's greatest social and economic historians, Michael Rostovtzeff. He writes of the social struggles of the Roman Empire and of the lessons we should learn from them: "Violent attempts at levelling have never helped to uplift the masses. They have destroyed the upper classes, and resulted in accelerating the process of barbarization."[3]

Class: the Fragmentation of Mankind. Although class struggle certainly did take place in human history before Marx and Engels, it was they who called it the moving power in human development and saw in it the motor of progress. They saw human society divided according to one principle: into the exploited and the exploiting classes. Government and religion, according to them, are the tools of the exploiters to maintain themselves in power and the exploited in docile obedience. According to their theory,

[3] Michael Rostovtzeff, *The Social and Economic History of the Roman Empire,* 2nd ed. (Oxford: Oxford University Press, 1957), Vol. I, p. 541. As a White Russian, Rostovtzeff may have had some personal reasons for feeling this way, but his observation remains true for ancient Rome— and for modern Russia.

the class struggle between oppressors and oppressed will eventually result in the victorious revolt of the largest and most oppressed class, the proletariat. The dictatorship of the proletariat will in turn give place to the classless society.

In one sense, struggle on the part of the oppressed against their oppressors is looked upon by Marxist theory as inevitable and unavoidable; in another sense, it is not inevitable, for it has to be promoted and encouraged. The lethargy of masses who are too blunted in their sensitivity (or perhaps too satisfied if they live in an industrialized Western nation) to throw themselves fully into a class struggle must be overcome: they must be instilled with resentment and with revolutionary enthusiasm.

The Marxist view of human society—one which is shared theoretically or practically by many non-Marxists—is one of fragmentation. The organization of society, of private ownership, divides men and erects oppressive and unjust barriers between them. The existence of such barriers is plain enough. It is less plain that when the unjust social structures have been overthrown, a new and classless society will arise, in which justice will finally be possible because the possibility of exploitation will have been taken out of the hands of the individuals and classes that abused it. The Marxist error is to think that selfishness and greed are a *class* problem, not a *human* one.

In human experience—and the Russian revolution is now over half a century old—the destruction of the oppressor classes (the aristocracy and the middle class) and of their tools for oppression, their government and economic system, has not produced a classless society without oppressors and oppressed: it has merely produced different classes and new oppressors. The failure of the Marxist theory as applied in the U.S.S.R. and elsewhere has led some to reject the theory; others merely claim that it has never been properly applied: they say that the Russians are "revisionists," and that only Mao or Fidel Castro (or perhaps Daniel Cohn-Bendit) can be relied upon as a true interpreter of Marx. Whether the societies which Mao and Fidel Castro are producing or the one which a Cohn-Bendit could produce would ever be free of oppressors and oppression is a possibility about which the reader may speculate, if common sense and knowledge of human nature do not immediately give him the answer.

There is a fundamental difference between Rostovtzeff and the Marxists. Rostovtzeff, speaking as a historian, has told us what actually has happened in history when an upper, ruling, "oppressor" class was destroyed. Instead of justice, the society was plunged into barbarism. Marx and his followers, more philosophers than historians, suppose that something quite different will happen. This is a supposition which cannot be justified on the basis of any observation about what actually has happened in the past, but only on a basis of a certain faith, a faith in the essential goodness of man. As Bertrand Russell pointed out, Karl Marx (like Communists generally, in their official statements) displayed an optimism about man which really could be substantiated only by a belief in Providence—which for Marx of course did not exist.[4] It is a fact that Marxism, having repudiated the God of Israel and of the Christians, still believes in *progress*, which has caused many to call communism a *Christian* heresy. Christianity and Judaism have a linear concept of history: it moves in one direction and does not repeat itself, and therefore progress, "forward motion," is possible. Non-biblical views

---

[4] Bertrand Russell, *History of Western Philosophy* (London: Allen and Unwin, 1946), p. 816. Psychologist Arnold Kuenzli of Basel says that in Marx's emotional life, the revolution took the place of the Second Coming.

of history with neither beginning (Creation) nor end (Last Judgment), especially those of ancient Greek and modern Indian thought with their eternally repeating cycles, logically have no room for a concept of progress. Since Marxism believes in "progress," it is related to Christianity, but it is an empty hope, for it does not have a God to bring it about.

In any event, the objective historian finds it hard to accept the idea that eliminating a certain class of people will uplift the others. It takes a special kind of faith to believe that, namely, faith in the innate goodness of man in general and in the idea that evil can be quarantined within one class.

The optimism of Marxists in particular and of Liberals in general[5] about the goodness of man does not correspond very well to human reality, with all the evils which men perpetrate on each other. Both groups have sought to explain it by splitting off from mankind as a whole a limited group of bad men, to whom their optimism and its solutions do not apply. The Marxists from the first have proclaimed all-out class war as the means to destroy the bad oppressors. The Liberals, by contrast, would by no means physically destroy a whole class, as the Russian Communists did to their kulaks. They would prefer to reeducate it out of existence, supplementing the persuasion by economic measures, chiefly by highly progressive

[5] Liberals, whether "old Liberals" of the type who wanted as little government as possible, or "Liberals" as defined by M. Stanton Evans in *The Liberal Establishment* (New York: Devin-Adair, 1965), who want increasing government direction of society, share with the Marxists whom they oppose the fatal fallacy that man can be made good by improving his environment. Jesus Christ expressed a different view: "That which proceeds out of the man, that is what defiles the man. For from within, out of the heart of men, proceed the evil thoughts and fornications, thefts, murders, adulteries, deeds of coveting and wickedness, as well as deceit, sensuality, envy, slander, pride, and foolishness. All these evil things proceed from within and defile the man" (MARK 7:20–23).

tax rates and other means capable of squeezing it into oblivion. For our purposes, the important thing is not *how* the possessing classes are to be eliminated, whether by bloody revolution or slow evolution, but the shared optimism that once a certain class of oppressors has been "liquidated" or even merely "reeducated," the rest of mankind will begin to function in natural goodness.

The Liberals of twenty-five years ago made the same mistake with Hitler. United States' policy in 1941–45 was based on the theory that all human evil was concentrated in the Germans (the more consistent Liberals said "in the Nazis"). Thus it was felt that when Germany had been crushed, an era of perpetual peace would come. Churchill, who was no Liberal, saw the fallacy in this, but he could not convince Roosevelt, whose own Liberal optimism was fanned by elements of pro-Russian romanticism and by downright pro-Communist inclinations among his entourage.

Needless to say, human history teaches us in countless lessons the fallacy of believing that one group or one individual is the source of all evil. Writing shortly before the end of World War II, Denis de Rougemont predicted that with Hitler out of the way, men would cease to fear the devil, having thought that Hitler was the devil and he was finished. De Rougemont warned that the reappearance of evil on a massive scale would catch us by surprise, and indeed it did.[6]

As a widely observed phenomenon, the class struggle is indeed a central political reality. As long as human beings have even a measure of economic liberty, classes will begin to form. As long as absolute tyranny does not rule, the less fortunate class will struggle to rise. Until the rich

6 Denis de Rougemont, *La part du diable* (Neuchâtel: La Baconnière, 1945), pp. 58ff.

become unselfish and generous, they will struggle to preserve their privilege. Thus some form of class struggle will always exist as long as people have differing abilities, motivation, and advantages. As a nearly universal phenomenon, the class struggle must be acknowledged. As a principle or even worse, as *the* principle which leads to progress and justice, the class struggle is not merely inadequate: it is self-defeating. Selfishness and the tendency to exploit others are not confined to any one segment of mankind. Eliminating a class will not eliminate injustice, because men in general, and not a particular class of men, are responsible for injustice. It is "from within" that evil comes, "out of the heart of *men*" (MARK 7:21), and not the heart of capitalists, or of Nazis, or of Jews, or of Communists, or of Negroes—or even of army generals, Black Power people, and white racists, our latest popular scapegoats.

No single class or racial or cultural group can be the carrier of evil, and so eliminating a class or race or culture can never root out evil. A single class can, however, be the carrier of civilization, and destroying a particular class *can* lead to barbarism. It has done so in the past, as Rostovtzeff and all other historians can testify. This is a danger which should cause us to take much thought. Class struggle cannot bring the millennium, but it could bring back barbarism.

Human Solidarity. The observers of the class struggle are right in thinking that it is caused by evil humans, but they make a fatal error in thinking that human evil is ever to be found on one side only, that is, within a particular class. The fragmentation of the human race, placing the responsibility for social or economic evil on one class or group and calling the other innocent, which char-

acterizes the Marxist concept of the class struggle, is shared
by many non-Marxist groups, together with the dangerous
fallacy that eliminating the evil class or group will bring
a reign of peace and justice to society. Over against this
fragmentation, the biblical view of man places the doctrine of human solidarity.

Religious "Class Distinctions." Both Christians and Jews
have tended, like the rest of mankind, to think in terms of
classes ("Jews and Gentiles," "Christians and pagans,"
"saved and unsaved," etc.) and this tendency has been
called self-righteousness, hypocrisy, and worse. Two things
must be noted when talking about biblical "class distinctions." The first is that the Bible teaches human solidarity
before God in a drastic way, i.e., in terms of responsibility
and guilt, "*All* have sinned," writes St. Paul, "and fall
short of the glory of God" (ROMANS 3:23). The Old Testament too teaches that all mankind is in rebellion against
God; St. Paul bases his own argument in Romans 3 on the
Old Testament Psalms (PSALMS 14:1–3, 53:1–4, 5:9,
140:3, etc.). If Israel had a special position (and it did),
if it was God's Chosen People, it was not chosen because
it was special, but special because it was chosen. The New
Testament is much more clearly universal than the Old
in its offer of God's grace, but even the Old Testament
knew of human solidarity in terms of responsibility. Certainly the Old knew that the Chosen People sinned as did
others, and promised them a strict accounting (cf. AMOS
3:1–2).

The second is that the "class" distinctions, at least from
the New Testament onward, are *moral*, based on personal
conversion and faith. The class struggle concept of Marxism seeks to wipe out the evil class, the exploiters, by class
war, and hopes that the survivors, the formerly "op-

pressed," will be just and good. It fails because it over-looks or deliberately disregards the fact that the "op-pressed" have just as great an innate tendency to evil as their "oppressors," and that the experience of class war gives them plenty of opportunity to exercise it. The "class distinction" of Christianity seeks to eliminate the "evil class," the unbelievers, but not by war, but by persuasion and conversion. Where the process is successful, the class which remains, that of the believers, is not free of tend-encies to evil any more than the "oppressed" of Marxist theory, but the experience of conversion and the changed orientation which accompanies it will in theory give be-lievers the will and the weapons with which to combat those tendencies. Christian faith tells the convert that he must struggle with sinful impulses within himself, and pro-vides much practical help along the way. This is no perfect solution, but at least it does work to some extent, as the im-pact of Christian revivals on social conditions can attest.

Christianity, then, does not seek a solution to evil in human society by *purging* society of its "evil" members, whether they be thought of as a race, as by the Nazis, or as a class, as by the Communists. It recognizes the frag-mentation of mankind into bitter factions, but sees these not as the cause of human evil, but as the result of it, as the result of man's rebellion against God. It affirms the solidarity of mankind in this responsibility, and does not try to foist it all off on a particular class.

Men cannot escape from evil by wiping out a class or a group; the only escape is the overthrow of the reign of evil in the heart of the individual. Classes, races, and all other human groups consist of individuals, and individuals cannot remake society by being destroyed, impoverished, imprisoned, or controlled. Class struggle, which destroys some individuals together with their evil inclinations, will not help those who survive to overcome their own. Moral and spiritual struggle in the heart of an individual can overthrow the domination of evil in that individual; one individual can aid another, and moral health, like physical disease, can spread from person to person.

The doctrine of class struggle promises peace and justice for one class at the price of terrible suffering and injustice to another. The price has been paid many times over in today's world, but the promise is long in being fulfilled. The reason is simple: the source of evil lies not in the class, but in the individual. No Utopian scheme will work with man as he now is. Hitler recognized this, and wanted to breed a superrace; we have genetic planners today who go far beyond Hitler. More talented—and more tractable —men can certainly be bred, but can evil be eliminated by selective breeding? Never, as long as man remains human!

Dogma and Practice. The statement which has just been made has a dogmatic ring: it is a *necessary* and a *true* dogma, if in fact the message of Christ is true, for according to Him, all men need redemption. However often the phenomenon of class struggle may be observed, it cannot be taken by the Christian as the foundation for his thinking or as the principle for his action, for it denies both the solidarity of mankind and the worth of the individual man. Thus it perverts both biblical judgment and biblical grace. It perverts judgment by applying it only to a particular class and thereby denying implicitly that *all* have sinned. It perverts grace by teaching men to seek their salvation in changed class conditions, not in a changed human heart. It is in a real sense a truly *diabolical* doctrine, because, like the *diabolos* (the "accuser" or the "divider"), it divides men and sets them against each other.

An evil man can be overthrown by force, and the power of evil may be concentrated at a particular time in a certain political party or other group. In such circumstances, resistance or war may be necessary, perhaps even class war. But we must hold fast to the dogma, for it is true, that evil can never be conquered by destroying an external adversary. Evil can be conquered only at its source, only within "the heart of man," from which "proceed the evil thoughts." Perhaps the real tragedy of the short presidency of John F. Kennedy lies not in his brutal murder, but in the fact that although he had the gift of speaking to the hearts of men, and of inspiring individuals with hope and with noble sentiments, he dealt with classes and conditions and not with individuals. Before his murder, he seemed only to be manipulating the circumstances of American life, and not changing men. Perhaps, had he been spared, he could have fulfilled some of the hopes his noble words kindled in the hearts even of many who voted against him; perhaps he would have remained the prisoner of the mentality of our age, which sees men in terms only of classes and environmental conditions. The evil that proceeded from the heart of one individual has forever prevented us from knowing.

The doctrine of the solidarity of mankind and of the responsibility of the individual before God is basic to Christianity. The Christian is in the world; if Christianity is truth, he can help the world solve its problems only by bringing them into the light of that truth. He can never help it by taking refuge in speculations, whether they be those of the optimistic humanism of a Marx or of the cynical elitism of a Hitler. If the Christian is unwilling to bring human problems into the light of Christian truth, then he should give up his Christian faith, for Christ is either Lord of all, or Lord of nothing.

The Christian must preserve the light of Christian truth, or he has nothing to apply to the problems of mankind. But having preserved it, how is he to apply it? It is at this point that the crisis comes. The world, of which the Christian, the citizen of God's Kingdom, is also a citizen, is boiling. All is in turmoil, all is in flux. Even if God's truth is truth, and true for this world as well as for heaven, how can it be applied when walls are crashing and even the foundations are shaking everywhere?

The class struggle is *the* political phenomenon today. It is not the principle by which God seeks to redeem the world. On the contrary, it is the principle of the Divider, the Adversary, the Destroyer, the Diabolos, the one who is called "the god of this world" (II CORINTHIANS 4:4). The god of this world is blinding us, seeking to make us take the phenomenon, the class struggle, for the absolute reality, to make us take temporal things for eternal. We cannot accept the phenomenon as the fundamental reality, for to do so is to betray the One who is eternal and to make shipwreck of ourselves. It is a measure of the power of Satan as "god of this world" that his divisive tactics can seem to be the absolutely fundamental facts of human life. For those who do not know or will not trust the corrective furnished by biblical revelation, this principle of division and perpetual struggle seems to be ultimate reality. Appearance taken as reality is *to eidōlon*, the idol. To accept as ultimate a false principle, that which is apparent, artfully presented by the god of this world, instead of that which is real, revealed by the God who is God, is idolatry. The class struggle is an idea, not an idol of metal or stone, but just as the Moloch of the Phoenicians and the Carthaginians devoured their children, so this idea, though less substantial, has devoured those of our century. And so it will continue to do with unchecked vigor, if ever Christians faĺl into idolatry—the service of the idol, the image—rather than the real.

Idolatry. Idolatry involves taking something from the temporal horizon of human experience and calling it absolute, in other words, putting it in the place of God. But men usually do not hit on the idea of worshipping a thing, of calling it ultimate, unless it does have tremendous legitimate significance. Whether it be a fertility cult or a cult of the dead, human idolatries usually point to things which are deep and important realities in human life. The first task of a Christian as a Christian is to be faithful to the truth of the message which has been entrusted to him; the second task, and the one which confronts us here, is to understand the tremendous significance of the class struggle and the deep and important realities to which it points. We may not call them absolute in the sense that God is absolute, and they cannot redeem man or society, as the Gospel can. But they are aspects of the created world, which, though fallen, is real, and must be taken seriously. That will be our purpose in these pages.

2.

The Survival of the Fittest

THERE was a close relationship, at least in Karl Marx's eyes, between his teachings and those of Charles Darwin.[1] Although Darwin was unwilling to let Marx dedicate *Das Kapital* to him, as Marx wanted to do, his doctrine of the evolution of man by means of struggle for survival was taken over by Marx as a proof from natural science of Marx's theory of evolution in society by means of class struggle.

The general theory of evolution as the explanation for man as he exists today and for the rest of living things has been sharply criticized. It has been called a dogmatic faith based on a desire to believe it rather than a scientifically well-established theory based on good evidence. Even the most ardent scientific advocates of the theory have occasionally been forced to admit that there are some very substantial parts of it which have to be taken on faith without and sometimes even against evidence. The virtually complete triumph of evolutionary doctrine in both Communist and non-Communist countries seems to correspond as much to a desire to believe in inevitable

[1] Cf. R. E. D. Clark, *Darwin: Before and After* (Exeter, England: Paternoster Press, 1948), pp. 112f.

evolutionary progress as to the weight of the available evidence in favor of such progress. In his recent book, *Man's Origin, Man's Destiny*,[2] Professor A. N. Wilder Smith of the University of Illinois has drawn attention to the weaknesses in the theory and to the quasi-religious zeal with which it is promoted.

Wilder Smith writes as a proponent of the older, traditional Christian doctrine of special creation (that is, that the ancestors of the various living beings, including man, were individually or specially created by God in considerable variety; all evolution is not absolutely excluded, but it is not the chief cause of the existence and variety of living things and particularly is not the cause of man). He even opposes, both for scientific and for theological reasons, those who advocate "theistic" or divinely guided evolution.* Wilder Smith's views can be criticized as "Christian special pleading," but he is able to cite a number of other

---

[2] A. N. Wilder Smith, *Man's Origin, Man's Destiny* (Wheaton: Harold Shaw, 1968).

* It is an interesting fact that the general theory of evolution, which is presented as scientific truth in almost all primary and secondary schools, without any reference to the difficulties and objections raised by Wilder Smith, Kerkut, and others, is almost invariably taught in its materialistic form, i.e., as an explanation which makes God or a creative, divine intelligence absolutely unnecessary. The articles and essays on the origin of man or of living things which frequently appear in *Life* and other mass-circulation magazines are examples of this. Despite the fact that a significant number of scientists, both Christian and non-Christian, seem to believe that the theory of evolution requires a divine, creative intelligence behind it to make it work, this "theistic" implication to my knowledge never appears either in the popular, mass-media presentations or in the elementary and secondary school textbooks. In other words, while the facts supporting the evolutionary hypothesis do not necessarily point in an atheistic direction, but actually may point in a *theistic* one, this usually remains unsaid, so that the implications of evolution as taught in schools and as generally understood lead to the materialistic conclusions held by Marx. Just as Darwin furnished, against his will, the scientific basis for Marx's theories, so current elementary and high school teaching and mass-media presentations on human origins provide the logical justification for current human behavior by making class struggle the law of life.

eminent scientists, not committed to a religious position, who challenge the general theory of evolution or its antitheistic materialistic form.[3] Here we shall not consider these objections to the commonly accepted doctrine of evolution, although they are worth remembering. Instead, we shall turn to the theoretical implications and practical results of the doctrine of the survival of the fittest for the class struggle and for human values in general.

Struggle as the Pattern of Life. "Life is a battle, and whoever, in this world of eternal struggle, is not willing to fight, is unworthy of life." Those words came from the pen of Adolf Hitler. Hitler was also reported to have remarked in April 1945, as Germany was crumbling under the blows of vastly superior enemy forces, "The German people was not worthy of my great ideas. The future will belong to the stronger Slavic nation." Since Germany had failed, despite an almost superhuman exertion, to triumph in Hitler's "world of eternal struggle," he quite consistently wanted it consigned to destruction and oblivion, and in the last days of the war tried to destroy it completely. Needless to say, many on the Allied side, and not only the notorious Secretary of the U.S. Treasury, Henry Morgenthau, Jr., would have been happy to see Germany annihilated. Fortunately for mankind, and for the conscience of the victors, it did not happen. Germany and her ally Japan suffered greatly at the victors' hands, but were not destroyed. Perhaps all that they did suffer was deserved; nations which had behaved as Germany and Japan could well have expected even worse treatment. Nevertheless, the victors, at least the Western Allies, have developed

[3] Cf. Wilder Smith, *Man's Origin, Man's Destiny*, pp. 59ff. One significant example of criticism by a religiously uncommitted scientist is G. A. Kerkut, *Implications of Evolution* (London: Pergamon, 1960).

an uneasy conscience about certain things—the mass bombing of civilians, the use of atomic weapons, the war crimes trials, among others. How much worse our conscience would be had we turned against the Germans the extermination techniques which the Nazis devised for their "final solution to the Jewish problem"!

The mind rebels at the thought of exterminating a nation. And rightly so. Yet according to the presuppositions inherent in the concept of "the survival of the fittest," the German people, having failed to conquer, might properly have been destroyed. However dreadful this prospect is, it is well to look it in the face, because it is a logical and appropriate consequence of the concept that human progress comes from the struggle for survival. If the ability to win a ruthless struggle is the test of a man's or a nation's right to exist, then Germany—as well as a number of other nations—has forfeited it. Lest it be argued that the Germans fought very well against vastly superior adversaries (which they did), let it be said that knowing better than to pick on too many enemies at once also plays a role in being fit to survive!

Neither Christianity nor most other moral systems the world has known recognize the principle that the right to live belongs only to those who can defend it by force from their adversaries. According to Christianity (and to most of the other systems), every man has a right to live and can lose it only in case of extreme wrongdoing on his own part (e.g., by committing murder). Obviously the vast majority of humans find it easier and safer, if less exciting, to live under a system of Christian morality than of the struggle for survival. "Führer"-types, however, find it repressive. They cannot carry out their natural inclinations to subjugate the more numerous weaker members of their society. Thus Friedrich Nietzsche called Christianity a slave morality, a kind of conspiracy among the weak members of society to exalt love, mercy, kindness and pity in order to protect themselves from the strong. Too weak or cowardly to fight for survival, the Christians, he felt, preach brotherly love and thereby prevent truly lordly, powerful figures ("Supermen") from asserting themselves. Incidentally, they also keep the whole human race on a less noble and heroic level because its heroes are restrained, not encouraged. Swinburne and Edward Gibbon saw the decline of the glorious might of pagan Rome in somewhat the same terms. One question we should ask such men, however, is how *they* would have fared in a society of "heroic" violence and action. "Supermen," men of action, usually have little sympathy with philosophers, poets, and historians, unless they would clearly be useful to them as propagandists.

Essentially the argument for social change through class struggle does not seek a "heroic" form of society. In this respect, Mussolini and Hitler were more consistent followers of the Darwinian principle, according to which one would expect and approve the unrelenting subjugation of the weaker by the stronger. This may be in effect what really happens in Marxist society, as the Soviet repression of the Hungarian revolution and of the Czechoslovakian reforms showed, but it is not the theory. Class struggle is not intended, in Marxist eyes, to bring about the triumph of the stronger, but of justice and equity.

Justice through Class War? The Hitlerian form of the idea of the survival of the fittest has been thoroughly rejected. At least it has been rejected in its Nazi form, although similar racist ideas continue to reappear in different circles. Other forms of the survival-of-the-fittest doctrines are still with us. The old "robber-baron" idea of extreme economic individualism, which defends the right of the rich to become richer and expects the poorer and less efficient to perish, can also claim the support of Darwin, who was concerned about the way civilization does all that it can "to check the process of elimination; we build asylums for the imbecile, the maimed, and the sick; we institute poor-laws; and our medical men exert their utmost skill to save the life of everyone to the last moment."[4] Both traditional Western Liberal thought and Marxism reject, in theory at least, such a callous approach, and profess a genuine concern for the downtrodden, the oppressed, and the weak. The Marxist slogan, "From each according to his ability; to each according to his need," has a very humanitarian and quite anti-Darwinian ring. (It should perhaps be noted that in his personal life Darwin was a sensitive, tenderhearted man, and kind to animals. In this respect he was unlike Marx—and so were a number of notorious war criminals of World War II.)

The survival of the fittest, seen in such terms, by no means promotes social justice, unless justice is defined by the slogan, "Might makes right." In contrast to this maxim, there is a genuine humanitarian concern both in Marx and in Marxism. It is this concern, coupled with a passionate zeal for social justice, for the elimination of the rich and indolent oppressors of the poor, and for the uplifting of the humiliated and despondent, which attracts many sensitive people to the Marxist banner. Their moral sense impels them to fight against social injustice; Marxism, with its doctrine of the inevitability of its own triumph, "scientifically" guaranteed by the dialectic of history which Marx borrowed from Hegel, gives plausible "scientific"

4 Charles Darwin, *The Descent of Man and Selection in Relation to Sex: The Preservation of Favorite Races in the Struggle for Life*, 2nd ed. (New York: Collier, 1902), p. 180.

reasons why the triumph of social justice can be gained only by class war. Therefore the cause of Marxism appears not only right but also sure to win.

We have already noted the error in thinking that members of a particular group of people (rich landowners, Nazis) oppress others *because* they belong to that particular group, and that destroying the group or taking away its power will eliminate the fact of oppression. Actually, as Christian doctrine teaches and as general human experience should amply confirm, all men have a propensity to do evil, to oppress others.

The only sure way to eliminate all human oppression is to eliminate all humans. We observe, in fact, that Marxist revolutions, whether caused from within, as in Russia and China, or imposed from without, as in the "people's democracies" of Eastern Europe, can hardly be cited as eliminators of oppression. The tsarist government of Russia was no bourgeois democracy, but it had nothing on the scale of the mass deportations, the slave labor, and the total police surveillance of the Soviet Union. In pre–World War II Czechoslovakia, the minority Slovaks were somewhat underprivileged and the resident Hungarians and Sudeten Germans were even more so, but in Communist Czechoslovakia *everybody* is underprivileged, including the occupying Russian soldiers.

There are two major difficulties with the doctrine that social justice can be brought about through class struggle. The first involves a historical observation about what actually happens to society in a class struggle; the second is a psychological fact about what the means that are employed in revolution and civil war do to the people employing them. Rostovtzeff has already made the observation for the Roman Empire, and we have been able to make it for the Russians. Class struggle destroys the upper classes, but does not uplift the masses, and the elimination of the upper classes brings a society closer to barbarism. Certainly the former Russian Empire was a cruel and oppressive government, yet it seems hard to deny that the Communist dictatorship that succeeded has caused more suffering and been more oppressive than the government of the tsars. Today, of course, general living conditions in the Soviet Union are much better than in pre-1917 Russia, even though personal freedom remains very restricted. But how much of that is due to communism and the class struggle, and how much to the industrial and economic progress of the civilized world in general? The distribution of necessities and luxuries in Communist Russia is probably more equitable than in tsarist days. But the standard of living is lower than in many nonsocialist countries which in 1919 were no less backward than Russia. Can we speak of increasing social justice where there is so little personal freedom? Finally, on the level of historical observation, surely the mass deportation of national minorities, the slave-labor camps, and the condemnation of millions of small farmers (kulaks) to slow death by starvation can well be considered as examples of the barbarism of which Rostovtzeff warned.

The second major difficulty may be called *psychological* or *ethical*. It depends on the fact that, contrary to the motto, "The end justifies the means," in actual practice means shape their own ends. They also change the people who make use of them. Terror and oppression not only breed counterterror and counterviolence among the oppressed victims; they also affect those who perpetrate them. How difficult it is for a ruler or a regime that came to power by violence and that ruled by force and terror to turn aside from terror and oppression into ways of freedom! Pavel Tigrid, Czech journalist and author of "The Prague

Spring,"[5] suggests that even if the Soviet Union and its more faithful satellites had not invaded Czechoslovakia in August 1968, the hopes of the government of Alexander Dubček would have been doomed to failure. According to Tigrid, the government's desire to permit criticism and correction could not have been fulfilled within the limits prescribed by Marxism, according to which one party only, the Communist party, may determine the destiny of the state. Either Dubček would have had to yield the rising pluralistic tendencies, leading to a multi-party state and thus constituting in effect an abandonment of communism, or he would have had to resort again to government suppression of liberty. As things turned out, of course, the Russian invasion forestalled the consequences of the dilemma into which Dubček was leading Czechoslovak communism. If one does not consider pre-August 1968 Czechoslovakia as a truly sovereign state, i.e., as one which really was able to determine its own destiny without outside interference, then the Russian intervention is another example of how difficult it is for a power established by terror and force to permit their abandonment even in a small part of the total region under its control.

On the level of human psychology, it is hard for individuals who have been brutalized by violence and who have grown accustomed to exercising it to abandon it when the "class struggle" is over. The continuing vigilance towards "counterrevolutionaries," "revisionists," and "reactionaries," which is the watchword of "revolutionary" governments, even when they have been established for half a century and supposedly enjoy the confidence of all the people, shows this. If a man, or a government, has seized power by conspiracy, treachery, and violence, and has exterminated the opposition in a drastic manner, he

[5] *Le printemps de Prague* (Paris: Seuil, 1968).

inevitably suspects that there are others around ready to conspire against him, betray him, and do him violence.

The idea that class struggle can result in increased justice has never yet worked in history. That does not prove that it cannot work, but in order for it to work, a great transformation would have to take place among those who unchain it and wage it. Their brutalization would have to reverse itself. The fundamental problem remains that of the heart of man. Can a tyrant become a philanthropist? The oppressed classes, having destroyed their oppressors in the class struggle, bear in their own hearts the same evil propensity to become oppressors. This propensity is if anything increased by the experience in violence and terrorism which they gained in coming to power. Violence breeds violence, and struggle more struggle. In the fifty-odd years since the victory of the Communists in Russia, some of the most arbitrary and cruel aspects of that country's totalitarian regime have been modified, but we can hardly say that oppression has ceased. If there is no class struggle in Russia today, it is not because there are no class grievances, but because the new rulers do not take the chances that the tsars did. Victory in the class struggle does not create virtue: power corrupts, and the class struggle, which pushes for extremes, puts absolute power into the hands of the victors.

The Value of the Individual. The concept of the survival of the fittest or the class struggle, whether it leads us to think of "preferred races" (Darwin's term) or classes, has a fatal impact on the concepts of human dignity and the worth of the individual. Throughout all human experience and in every type of social and economic structure, certain individuals have been allowed to acquire or to inherit a better position, more power, greater wealth than others.

It has been the function of all governments to secure to
the individual members of society, including the less powerful and fortunate, a certain degree of security and freedom.
By democratic standards, a government which provides
greater protection and freedom to more people is a better
government than one which provides less or provides them
to fewer people.

The very existence of freedom for individuals will always
make it possible for some of them to advance in power,
wealth, and prestige by comparison with others. No society
at all can prevent this. What it can do is to provide a certain
fundamental minimum of dignity, of security, and of liberty
that it guarantees to all and protects for all. Such an
attempt to secure the dignity of every individual is consistent both with the Christian and with the humanistic
view of man. It obviously conflicts with the concept of the
survival of the fittest and with the idea that society pro-
gresses through class war. Ideally the class struggle should
result in the triumph of "the people," that is, of the
largest class. But it does so by trampling on those individuals who make up the upper and middle classes, and—
as we know—the dictatorship of the proletariat guarantees
neither great freedom nor great dignity for those individuals
who make up the proletariat.

We are all familiar with the terrible and abominable
crimes that have been perpetrated when a special dignity
or indignity has been associated with membership in a
particular race. But "classist" thinking, if we may coin
a word, is just as fatal to the dignity of the individual as
racist thinking. The individual who has the misfortune
to belong to the class which is out of favor suffers, but
even within the favored class the individual man or woman
enjoys no legal immunity or personal dignity.

In the bourgeois democracies, with their traditions of

more or less free economic development, people have learned to recognize and to fear the evil effects of an exaggerated individualism. But it is wrong to blame such effects on Christianity. Without denying that the Western nations where capitalism has flourished were nominally Christian and that this did not prevent them from producing "captains of industry" who behaved like robber barons, it is worth noting that the Manchester School, the proponent of extreme laissez faire capitalism, justified its theories, just like Marx, by an appeal to the doctrines of Charles Darwin. According to the German sociologist Max Weber and his English disciple R. H. Tawney, John Calvin and his Puritan descendants were the spiritual fathers of modern capitalism. This so-called "Weber-Tawney thesis" holds that Calvinism and Puritanism replaced spiritual discipline with this-worldly discipline, leading to the accumulation, investment, and re-investment of capital as a religious duty.[6] The Weber-Tawney thesis has become an unquestioned dogma of most sociologists and is used to discredit both capitalism and Calvinism, depending on the circumstances. In fact, however, both Weber and Tawney take their evidence not from Calvin and the Puritans, but from rationalistic, moralistic deists like Benjamin Franklin. The famous sociologist of religion Ernst Troeltsch has pointed out that all varieties of Christianity have considered material wealth a spiritual danger, one which could be overcome only by a strict doctrine of stewardship and rigorous accountability to God for the use made of this world's goods. The recent Conference on Faith and History held at Grand

[6] See Max Weber, *The Protestant Ethic and the Spirit of Capitalism* (New York: Scribner's, 1958), and R.H. Tawney, *Religion and the Rise of Capitalism* (London: Penguin, 1969), both reprints of much earlier editions. Edmund Opitz, in *Religion and Capitalism: Friends, Not Enemies* (New Rochelle: Arlington House, 1970), gives the credit for capitalism (which he praises) not to Calvinism but to Judaeo-Christian ethics in general.

Rapids, Michigan (October, 1971), has established once
again that both Calvin himself and his Puritan disciples
shared this very negative view of wealth and worldly ambi-
tion.[7]

That this has always or even usually prevented nominal
Christians from becoming economic tyrants cannot be said,
but that it has often induced Christian capitalists to use
their wealth in very altruistic ways also cannot be denied. It
can also be argued that the nominally Christian nations
where capitalism has flourished have incidentally done more
to raise living standards for all levels of society than other
systems, even though the industrialists did not have this
altruistic goal. Perhaps the reason for the rise of non-
Christian and anti-Christian movements for social justice,
like communism, lies not in the fact that Christianity
offered no solutions to the problems caused by the Industrial Revolution, but rather in the fact that in the early
nineteenth century the Christian churches were so weakened by rationalism that they lacked the confidence and
the enthusiasm to try to apply biblical moral principles to
the economic and social problems of their day. *In other
words, consistent Christian thinking was never brought to
bear on the issues.* If this is true, this is all the greater
reason for Christians today to proclaim a Christian standard
by which to deal with modern social and economic
problems. Enlightened rationalism is too weak, and communism too tyrannical, to promote social justice. Why not
try consistent Christianity?

The dangers of excessive individualism are still with
us, but the dangers of collectivism loom greater. The
socialist countries of the world deliberately reduce the
individual to a small and very expendable cog in a great

[7] Ernst Troeltsch's famous book, *The Social Teachings of the Christian
Church*, is also available in a paperback reprint (New York: Harper Torchbooks, 1956).

machine: to cannon fodder for the class warfare from which progress is supposed to come. In the nonsocialist countries, there are also many forces operating to reduce individual freedom and to incorporate individuals into vast and impersonal economic and social structures. It is against this danger that many of the New Left, especially among the student radicals, are protesting, and rightly so. Unfortunately, their total rejection of present social structures, if successful, would open the doors to a "revolutionary" tyranny, which would quickly use force and terror to accomplish the mechanization of mankind towards which our present economic and social development is drawing us in slow stages. If past history teaches us anything, the cure would be worse than the disease. One of the irrational paradoxes of the New Left is that it often advocates complete sexual anarchy in its revolt against all bourgeois standards and values, while at the same time claiming as its patron Mao Tse-tung, a man who has curtailed sexual expression more severely than any Puritan, in many cases forcing even husbands and wives to live in prolonged separation from each other.

There is no obstacle to spreading collectivism from within the mentality of class struggle, for it has no place for the individual. The Christian has many things with which to reproach the non-Christian humanist, who in effect substitutes man, or the secular humanist ideal of man, for God. They have something very important in common, however; they share a similar conception of the *solidarity* of mankind. The humanist thinks of man as unfallen, free, and capable of constant self-improvement. All of these attributes are questionable from the Christian point of view, but at least the humanist gives man these honors as *man*, and not as a member of the Nordic (or Negro) race, a proletarian, or as a businessman. The humanist, like the Christian, speaks of mankind as a whole and of men as individuals. This earns them both the charge of sentimentality, romanticism, and of adhering to a slave morality from those who think progress can come only by the struggle which fragments mankind into hostile classes or other groups. But the man who thinks in class terms always loses respect for individuals. It is significant that the widespread horror of capital punishment which has led to its abolition or virtual abolition in several Western countries is not shared in the socialist countries. If whole classes must be eliminated in the name of progress, it would be strange indeed to be very concerned about one human life.

Perhaps the Marxist view that progress comes through class struggle is in fact more directly related to the Hegelian view of history as a dialectic process than to the Darwinian view of the survival of the fittest. We have seen that both Marxism and Darwinism consider it natural and even inevitable to sacrifice all the members of the "oppressing" or "less fit" classes or races to the "oppressed" or the "fitter." If individual men, as men, can (and even ought to) be deprived of their individual rights because of the class to which they belong, then even those individuals who belong to the more favored group can and will also be sacrificed. The class struggle and the Darwinian evolutionary view of mankind have this in common: not only do they sacrifice individuals to the class and some classes to others in the present, but they sacrifice the whole of present mankind to the future.

Among the unexamined assumptions in the doctrine of the evolutionary progress of mankind, whether it is seen in dialectical or in biological terms, is the assumption that men of today can and should be willing to suffer for the future of the race. In other words, a certain altruism is expected of today's men and women for the sake of the hoped-for race of tomorrow. The difficulties of this position are many.

The altruism which makes a man willing to suffer and even to die for the sake of generations to come is explicable in traditional Christian or even humanistic terms, but it is a bit strange on the basis of survival-of-the-fittest thinking. The Christian has a confidence in his own security in God; he knows that God loves him and expects him to act in love; this makes personal sacrifice plausible since God will make it good to him at the consummation of the world and the Last Judgment. The humanist, of course, has no such hope, but his exaltation of individual human motivation and of the human race provides a plausible kind of rationale. If man is noble and if the human race is a thing of worth, a noble individual may naturally sacrifice himself for it. From the point of view of the survival of the fittest, however, such an attitude is self-defeating. The very altruism which makes a man sacrifice himself obviously constitutes unfitness, as it prevents him from surviving. By sacrificing himself he declares himself and his stock unfit and disinherits them for the future. Perhaps an awareness of this inconsistency is why communism and other future-oriented systems have never relied on altruistic self-sacrifice, but have always supplemented it with a considerable measure of coercion.

Another problem, of course, lies in the fact that the race of the future, for which this distant and phenomenal progress is hoped, is—if it makes the hoped-for progress—no longer the race which has suffered today. Just as it would have been quite peculiar for the Jews going to the gas chambers to have taken any comfort from the fact that their death was to pave the way for a better "master race," so it is difficult for *Homo sapiens* of the twentieth century to take much real comfort in the thought that planned biological and social evolution will breed a new race of twenty-fifth-century beings quite superior to himself. They will perhaps be happier than we, but we can take any comfort today in sacrificing our freedom and happiness so that a new and different race will not suffer as we have? A man may be happy in the thought that his sufferings will help his children, but the prospective future joy of a new and different race is a comfort which requires a strong imagination to appreciate. Goethe's Faust reached old age without ever having been satisfied by the pleasures, the power, or the excitement Mephistopheles had provided him in a long and marvelous life. As an old man, he claimed at the last that he finally experienced real fulfillment in anticipation of a land-reclamation project to benefit future ages:

> In anticipation of that highest joy,
>
> I *now* enjoy life's supreme moment.

For Faust, interestingly enough, that was the moment of his defeat: he had lost his wager to the devil, who came to claim him.*

As Eric Mascall has pointed out, the word "man" is often abused by those who use it "as if 'man' was some kind of enduring entity, whose misery at one time could be compensated by its prosperity some centuries later. It cannot be too strongly emphasized that apart from the theological sense . . . in which we are all one man in Adam and in Christ, there is no such being as *man*, there are only *men*; and no glorification of the evolutionary process and its inevitable direction can contradict the equally inevitable and

---

* In Goethe's fantastic allegory, angels came to deliver him, singing, "Who ever striving never rests, him we can save." This has become one of German secularism's most fundamental themes, although seldom is it directly expressed. The difference between Goethe's vision and that of the believer in evolutionary progress is that it was *Faust* himself who was saved by "ever striving," not a new race of super-Fausts of ages to come (*Faust*, II, lines 11585–86).

8 Eric L. Mascall, *The Secularisation of Christianity* (London: Darton, Longman, & Todd, 1965), p. 208.

far more obvious fact that it is the individual men who are born, toil, suffer, rejoice, love, hate, and in the end, die."[8] To sacrifice the men of today for the men of the future is no more moral than to sacrifice the Jews of 1944 for the Germans of that year, or the bourgeois of today for the proletariat of today.

However useful class thinking may be for purposes of sociological analysis, or to inspire certain classes to promote and others to permit necessary social change, if carried to its conclusion, if it becomes a principle to be followed instead of a phenomenon to be understood and dealt with it destroys the individual. And we are individuals, we are not "man." What does it profit a man if historical evolution goes triumphantly on, and he himself is ground under?

Implications of Justice. It has been said repeatedly that both the class struggle as a principle and the evolutionary faith in progress fail to do justice and to give dignity to the individual men and women who are alive today, that instead they sacrifice the present to a future which may never come (if Rostovtzeff is right), and which will not be *our* future if it comes (and Darwin is right). The use of the criteria of justice and dignity for those who are alive today is necessary as a foundation for justice and dignity for those who will live tomorrow. Just as the individual may not excuse evil actions today because of an intention to perform good actions in the future, so society may not excuse injustice committed today on the grounds of justice planned for tomorrow. The evil that men do lives after them: the evil of Negro slavery, which was abolished in 1865, still continues to weigh heavy on the United States and to frustrate hopes of racial justice and harmony more than a century later.

Ethical obligations speak to man *now*. Just as the commands of God are addressed to man in his present, so human misery and degradation cry out their pleas in the present imperative: "Help me!" never, "Get ready to help my descendants!" The contemporaneity, the now-ness of ethical obligations, disqualifies the class-struggle concept because it perpetuates or even multiplies injustice, not to classes, but to men.

What are we to say of the present situation, of the existing order in our still nonsocialist world? Together with a measure of security and personal freedom, it perpetuates and may even multiply certain injustices. We do well to avoid the pitfalls of class-struggle slogans, but we must remember that if class struggle is not the *cure* for injustice, it is very tangible *evidence* that there *is* injustice, and that in some ways it is built into the structures of our society. Justice is a two-edged sword. We must not be afraid to use it, in the name of living men, against the blind and brutal doctrine of class struggle. But then we must also be willing to let it cut out the evils in our own social order. That may be painful, but it will be less painful and more just than the alternative. It is not enough to see the dangers inherent in the advocacy of class struggle; we must also try to resolve those real problems which give rise to it. In order to do so, it will be necessary to look at the different varieties of class struggle which exist in the world today.

3.

Industrialists and Proletarians: Economic Classes

IN its classical form, the idea of the class struggle conceives of classes in economic terms. As a concept, it only arose with the Industrial Revolution and the emergence of the European proletariat. In Marxist thinking, the emergence of the proletariat—the vast group of wage earners created by the rise of industrialism—was a decisive step in the history of human thought.[1] It was not until the necessary social environment came into being, according to this theory, as factories arose and the independent craftsman-artisan gave way to the factory worker who hired himself out to the factory owner, that "thought itself" could become the province of the working masses rather than of the aristocracy and the bourgeoisie. This collectivization of thought, if we may speak thus, made it possible for thought itself to escape from an unscientific, romantic individualism and to come to grips with the life-forces of social evolution, in a word, with the class struggle. The reader who knows of Teilhard de Chardin's concept of the growth of the

[1] *Marxistische Philosophie, Lehrbuch,* ed. Alfred Kosing (East Berlin: Dietz, 1967), pp. 45ff.

noosphere (sphere of the mind, from Greek *nous*, mind) to embrace the whole globe will see a certain parallel here.

There is no doubt that the rise of the industrial proletariat has coincided with a kind of collectivization of thought. Whether the one caused the other, of course, may be a different question. The improvement of schools and the spread of compulsory education, the increase in literacy, and finally the advent of the mass media (first newspaper, then radio, film, and television) have certainly made thought, its communication, and its fixation for posterity far more widespread than before. In a sense perhaps different from that of Teilhard, a noosphere, a layer of thought, has spread itself over our globe in recent decades. In a general way, knowledge of political, economic, and intellectual issues is no longer confined to an upper or intellectual class. Events which take place in the morning anywhere on the globe can be known, discussed, and reacted to all over the world by that evening.

The universality and the rapidity of communication make it possible for ideologics to develop and to motivate large masses of people to good or evil ends. Mass media can work or be exploited to propaganda ends. Because of the refractory nature of man, propaganda campaigns do not always produce the desired effect. For example, the government-sponsored antismoking campaigns can hardly be called a total success. It is not altogether clear that bringing political, economic, and intellectual issues to the attention of the masses and prodding or permitting them to react to them are necessarily a step forward for civilization.

Captain Richard Grenfell of the Royal Navy has pointed out how the systematic exploitation of mass media by the Allies in World War I, utilized in order to rouse the people to a greater war effort, had so embittered public opinion in the Allied nations that the cruel and illegal hunger blockade of defeated Germany was popularly accepted in 1919 and that it was psychologically impossible for the Allies to write a reasonable peace treaty at Versailles in 1919. The legacy of Versailles, which included Adolf Hitler and World War II, was in some measure the legacy of the exploitation of the mass media by the Allied governments.[2] The victor's justice of Nuremberg, which has in recent years come home to plague the once victorious Western Allies of 1945, was to no small degree inevitable in view of the tremendously inflamed state of public opinion against the Germans. Had the Western democracies, like Russia, had a controlled press, instead of merely an influenced one, they could doubtless have quickly calmed public hostility to the defeated Axis powers, had they so wished. But in general the free press of the West (and to some extent even the publicly managed media of radio and television in certain Western countries) follows its own laws, which are not necessarily determined by considerations of government policy and interest. The "democratization" of thought in this sense is not an unmixed blessing.

The spread of political consciousness on the level of the masses, and the fact that they have the ability and the will to react to it, is manifesting itself in all the major Western nations and to a certain extent in the "people's democracies," although apparently not in Russia. This makes it possible for segments of the population to become violently agitated about real issues, which in earlier times would have been long in coming to a head, and even about petty or artificially created problems. The ability of the masses or of a particular class to react at once to any one of a variety of stimuli has also contributed to the development of what the Germans call the A.P.O. (*ausserparlamentarische Opposition*), the extra-parliamentary opposition.

[2] Cf. Richard Grenfell, *Unconditional Hatred: German War Guilt and the Future of Europe* (New York: Devin-Adair, 1954).

The industrial proletariat is characterized by the fact that its members, unlike free craftsmen, do not own their means of production, in the operation of which they spend their lives and expend their strengths. It is fairly obvious that although a factory hand invests the years of his life and the sweat of his brow just as does the craftsman, the storekeeper, or the businessman, the factory hand, if he gains only a living wage, does not build up an investment like the owner of a workshop or a business. The large concentrations of an industrialized economy can be much more productive than small artisan-industry, but they are also more subject to economic dislocation; the factory with too few orders becomes unprofitable. It may close and therefore pay its workers nothing; a small smith, by contrast, can survive for a long time with too little work to live well but enough to keep from starving. The factory worker with no share in the enterprise in which he works is much more vulnerable. Ownership of the means of production, or a share in such ownership, obviously becomes increasingly important as production becomes more and more centralized. A true industrial proletariat, to be open to the class struggle, must have a consciousness of its lack of economic power and must sense the fact that it is at the mercy of blind or indifferent economic powers. The late nineteenth and early twentieth century provided this situation, and the workers were made increasingly conscious of it by the rise of mass media.

Means of Production. Ownership of the means of production is quite evidently a vital factor in the life of people living in any economic system in which production is highly organized. If we assert that Christian ethics are meant to be applied today, then we must be able to explain how they relate to the concept of ownership of the means of production.

At first glance the principles laid down in the Old Testament might seem quite ill-suited to serve in an industrial society, because they bear the stamp of conditions in a nomadic culture and of very early urban societies, based on trade and crafts with but little productivity as such. The world of Jesus in the New Testament likewise reflects a limited social and economic horizon. Even if we accept the supposition that St. Joseph, as a carpenter, was really a kind of entrepreneur, and that Jonas, the father of Peter and Andrew, and Zebedee, the father of James and John, were commercial fishermen with a business of a certain size (they had hired employees), we still have the picture of a very circumscribed economic milieu, hardly in touch with the great world of commerce, banking, and industry.

When we consider the Acts of the Apostles, however, the picture is already a bit broader. Peter is in a position to mix socially with junior Roman officers (ACTS 10), and the evangelist Luke is evidently a man of considerable breadth of experience and culture. Yet it is with Paul that broad vistas open: a Roman citizen, he seems to have been at home in commerce despite his trade of tentmaker; it is hard to explain the ease and familiarity with which he voyaged from one end of the Roman world to the other, the natural way he booked passages on shipboard, the ready contact he had with imperial and local officials, unless we think of him as having a good background in the world of affairs of his day. His writings and speeches show at least some knowledge of Greek literature, and chapter 1 of his Epistle to the Romans suggests that he was familiar not only with Roman but with Egyptian paganism. Paul's cultural status so evidently put him on a level with his great Roman contemporary, the fabulously wealthy philosopher and capitalist Seneca, the tutor of Nero, that a fictitious exchange of letters was composed in their names.

Nevertheless, despite Paul's undoubted opportunity to

know something of the commercial life of the Roman world, we do not find that his epistles introduce significant new elements, by comparison with the Old Testament and with Jesus, concerning the ethics of economic life, and particularly concerning the means of production. The same two points of contact are present; a third concept, possibly relevant too, is introduced in his second Thessalonian epistle.

The New Testament, in common with the Old, recognizes and takes for granted the right to private ownership of property. The commandment against stealing in the Old Testament Decalogue is but the most outstanding of a number of instances. The rights of the government to exact taxes and to compel military service and even forced labor are also taken for granted, although abusive exactions are clearly seen as an evil. Characteristically, the taking of interest on loans made to those in distress is forbidden (EXODUS 22:25), and foreclosure of debts to amass property and the exploitation of the poor are severely condemned (e.g., AMOS 4:1 ff., 8:5–6). The "sacred right" to private property, which some economic conservatives triumphantly see in the Bible, certainly is there, or at least it is very strongly implied. But certain other things are implied as well which are ill-suited to our present economic order, such as the extreme limitations on the right to exact interest for loans; this would seriously hamper our present economic system, which certainly depends on the legitimacy of a return on a loan or investment without regard to the possible need of the borrower or to the sacrifice he may have to make to repay it.

In any case it is clear that the right of a man to acquire and possess goods and land is presupposed and protected in the Bible. In a sense we can even say that possession of private property is an *absolute right*, but we have to add immediately that hospitality and generosity to those in need, even to travelers, are then *absolute duties* and dare not be neglected.

SLAVERY AND THE BIBLE

How do things stand with "the means of production"? In biblical days the means were limited. A small workshop could obviously be owned by the master craftsman. The most significant means of production in antiquity which could be owned consisted of human slaves. Human slavery, a familiar phenomenon in the history of almost every society, was widespread in antiquity; it was a more or less natural consequence of the capture of prisoners in battle. The New Testament recognizes it to the extent of tolerating it and not attempting to abolish it. That alone is a remarkable fact, and one which alarms and embarrasses Christians when they face it. The Old Testament goes further: it expressly permits slavery (see e.g., LEVITICUS 25:44–46). Non-Jews, at least, might be owned as slaves; Jews who sold themselves to their fellow Jews to pay their debts had to be released after a certain period.

The permission given in the Old Testament to own slaves, something which to us seems grossly immoral, appears all the more perplexing in the light of the frequent Old Testament stipulation that Jews and strangers must have the same treatment in the eyes of the law, a generous principle which the United States government does not entirely follow. Of course, slaves, according to both the Old and the New Testaments, were to be considered as brothers by their owners, if the slaves also were Jewish, or in the New Testament, Christian. From our twentieth-century perspective we find it difficult to understand this tolerance of an all too common affront to the dignity of man. How could God permit human slavery?

To be sure, slavery in the Old Testament and in the Roman world was not *necessarily* terrible. Slaves could enjoy many rights, possess vast powers, gain wealth, and in some cases buy their freedom. Some of ancient Rome's most famous figures were freedmen. The lot of a slave in pagan Rome was usually much more bearable and promising than that of a slave in the "Christian" American South before 1865. (Of course the lot of the mining slaves was dreadful.) None of these factors can excuse, most of us would feel, the permission for or even the mere toleration of as cruel and oppressive an institution as that of slavery. It is true that within the Christian world, slavery gradually was abolished. But we must emphasize the *gradually*. It took almost 1,500 years from the establishment of Christianity within the Roman Empire in 380 to the abolition of slavery in the United States with the defeat of the Confederacy in 1865. Since Islam is six hundred years younger (three hundred as an established religion), Christians have no right to be supercilious about the persistence of slavery in the Moslem world.*

The tolerance expressed by the New Testament towards

---

* The readiness of men to make slaves of other men has not been overcome by twentieth-century "progress," as is shown by the slave-labor camps which existed in Nazi Germany and which still exist in Soviet Russia. The fact that such slaves have in some cases been condemned by courts and are "owned" by the government, not by private masters, does not make them any the less slaves. The largest slaveowner of ancient Rome was the Emperor, just as the largest slaveholder in Europe today is the Russian government. Even the Western Allies, the United States, Britain, and France, agreed to use captured German soldiers for forced labor as "reparations"—a thing contrary to the rules of war and not significantly different from classical slavery. The United States, having qualms about using prisoners in such fashion, turned a large number of its captives over to France which exploited them for about two years. Many German and Japanese prisoners were still being held by the Russians a decade after the war's end. It was customary to speak of German use of "slave labor" during World War II, but to be consistent we should speak of Allied use of "slaves" as well.

an institution like slavery does not prove that God approves of it. *It does prove that the Christian has no Christian mandate for violent social change.* If there was no call to first-century Christians to free their own slaves, much less to revolt to abolish slavery everywhere, certainly we must be hesitant about saying that Christ would have his twentieth-century disciples engage in revolutionary violence to overthrow what are clearly lesser social evils than slavery. (Here again the problem becomes complicated: perhaps the underprivileged denizens of underdeveloped regions actually live today in greater misery and degradation than a typical first-century slave did. Conceivably the difference could be great enough to justify action now which was not justified then.) It would also seem to show, since the slaves of that day were the means of production, that means of production could be left in private hands. This is admittedly a somewhat distant inference from the economic situation of that day to ours, but at least it indicates that here too private ownership is not necessarily to be rejected.

Neither of these two principles, derived from the economic situation which was accepted if not approved by the New Testament, offers much guidance for building up a positive Christian program for the current situation, dominated, as we all know, by the specter of class struggle. Neither the extreme diffidence of Jesus and the Apostles towards revolutionary violence nor the inferred principle that since slaves might be privately owned, factories may also be, is much of a positive guide. Our twentieth-century society seems to require more definite principles. Both the nonrevolutionary attitude of the first Christians and their tolerance of or submission to slavery do clearly show us one thing, however: in Christian perspective, the outward structures of society and of economics are not crucial for man: what is crucial, salvation, can be achieved in spite of them or in disregard of them. Man's dignity does not depend primarily on economic freedom.

If we are to draw a positive lesson from the undeniable fact that both the Old and New Testaments require humane and dignified treatment of slaves but do not require laws against the inhumane and degrading institution of slavery, it is that personal relationships are more important for time and eternity than are legal structures. (A well-known Negro, active in New York Democratic politics, told this writer before the 1960 presidential conventions that he would support Johnson, at that time still known as an advocate of segregation, but would not support a rival Democrat who was a standard bearer of integration. Johnson, he said, though a segregationist, would treat a Negro as a man, whereas his integrationist rivals often treated him only as a voting bloc, disdaining him as a man. Perhaps the completeness of President Johnson's conversion to the cause of racial equality stems from the fact that he had always had good personal relationships with Negroes, even when still a declared Texas segregationist.)

The strange reticence of Christianity in the face of a great and obvious social evil and inequity such as slavery embarrasses us. Yet, if on the one hand we accept Christ as our Pattern and the teachings of His Apostles as authoritative, and on the other recognize human servitude as a terribly cruel, degrading, and evil thing, which it is, this strange reticence to take steps to change the structures of society will show us one thing with vivid clarity. When Jesus preached, "Seek ye first the kingdom of God, and his righteousness" (MATTHEW 6:33), He really meant *first*. Terrible as human servitude to a cruel master in this life is, how much more terrible must be eternal servitude to the master of darkness! From this comes Jesus' insistent, mysterious *first*. He came to set men free, but they needed freedom first of all as "those who through fear of death were subject to slavery all their lives" (HEBREWS 2:15). Even to free men from the yoke of physical slavery in this world is less pressing than the task of freeing them from the power of death.

The long history of Christianity is not destitute of real triumphs in the realm of social amelioration, but it is not rich in them either. If the reason were that the church had, in fact, always put first things first, there would be no shame in this comparative poverty. The misery of the church lies in the fact that it has often ignored the first things as much as the second.

As a French socialist remarked during the French crisis of May and June 1968, with its long general strike, "Neither a government of the Right nor a government of the Left can distribute what has not been produced." One of the curious ironies of twentieth-century history is that the dictatorships of the proletariat have left their "dictators," if not in actual want, at least habituated to a chronic scarcity of desirable consumer goods, while the "capitalist" economies, supposedly dedicated chiefly to the enrichment of the rich industrialists and putting the workers off with hopes of heaven, have in fact made more of this world's goods available to more people by far than their socialist rivals.

This is a comparison so obvious as to be almost ridiculous, yet it is not taken seriously. Perhaps the French workers showed that they were aware of it by their attitude during the spring crisis of 1968. Although a very high percentage of French industrial workers habitually vote Communist, and though the French "free enterprise"* economy has been slow to raise the living standards of the workers, they

* Of course, the French "capitalist" economy has certain peculiar problems of its own, involving a high degree of complexity and government interference. It is not a very good example of a free capitalist system.

did not respond to the appeal of the student radicals to overthrow the Fifth Republic. Instead they contented themselves with taking advantage of the turmoil to obtain some long overdue social and economic concessions. They felt, evidently, that a bourgeois bird in the hand was worth two Communist turkeys in the bush.

The comparison between East and West Germany, for example, is glaring. Prior to 1939, industrialized Czechoslovakia was economically much better off than Austria. Since World War II, even under its characteristically *gemütlich* and inefficient blend of socialism and free enterprise, Austria has climbed to a position of general economic well-being far superior to that of Czechoslovakia, a Communist state since the coup d'état of 1948. As late as 1967, even mildly anti-Communist Czechs were still explaining the obvious economic lethargy of their country in terms of the damage caused during the German occupation, 1939–1945. Of course, that occupation did not destroy nearly as much of Czechoslovakia's economic potential as did Allied bombing, land fighting and the dismantling of surviving plants as reparations in Germany.

It is probably impossible to demonstrate beyond any doubt that the Communist system is responsible for the relative poverty of the consumers in Eastern Europe. The starting points were different, and at the end of World War II their "benefactor," the Soviet Union, was not only unable to supply anything like the Marshall Plan aid provided by the U.S.A. to Western Europe; it actually exploited their economies and retarded their recovery. Nevertheless, it is hard to escape the conviction that the material prosperity of every level of society has increased far more rapidly in the bourgeois democracies than in the so-called people's democracies. It is an awareness of this fact which underlies the new direction taken by left-wing student agitation: protest against the "consumer society." Daniel Cohn-Bendit even allowed himself to cry out at a May demonstration, "Man shall not live by bread alone!"*

It is indeed a curious turn when the adherents of Marx, who for so long condemned bourgeois society for keeping its workers in check by offering them only "spiritual" values, reserving the good, solid material values for the exploiter, now cry out in rage that the consumer society showers men with things but destroys their spirits. It is more curious still that the charge is true. The consumer society is showering material blessings on all its members. It is easy to conclude that the free enterprise system is more productive by a large margin than communism.

The profit motive and the need to compete effectively or go under supply necessary incentives for efficiency at all levels of planning and management. But even if communism —or perhaps in this context we should call it state capitalism —should succeed in overcoming its perennial production problems, a significant handicap to consumer satisfaction would still exist: distribution. Can the centrally organized bureaucratic state outlets ever compete with the profit-hungry and customer-conscious local merchant in delivering the goods to the people who want them, or in selling them to people who do not yet know that they want them? Anyone who has ever visited a "people's democracy" will agree that the substitution of central planning for independent initiative appears to be the source of endless bottlenecks. Even if the goods are available, they can be very slow indeed in reaching those who want them.

---

* A young Protestant minister who was present challenged him, "Finish the sentence!" When Cohn-Bendit refused to do so, the minister did it for him, "but by every word that proceeds from the mouth of God" (MATTHEW 4:4, quoted by Jesus from DEUTERONOMY 8:3). This scene was reported to me by a Lausanne journalist who witnessed it.

But where both production and distribution function effectively, where all but the most stubbornly poor members of society are growing rapidly richer, what happens to economic class conflict, which theoretically is so important to social progress? Is it possible that the formerly oppressed classes will, in effect, be bought off by prosperity? Marx and Engels never envisaged the present situation. Their appeal was to eliminate the class which was taking the lion's share of the gross social product, and to distribute that lion's share among the workers. But they never imagined the possibility of an increase in productivity so spectacular that even the workers would no longer know what to do with their goods. They certainly did not expect that the day would come in which workers would begin to own shares in their own and other enterprises, and thus gradually turn from the oppressed into the oppressors!

When the distribution of this world's goods becomes so liberal that it includes not merely homes and cars, television sets and tape recorders, vacations in summer and skiing in winter but also industrial shares for an increasing percentage of the erstwhile proletariat, the principle of the class struggle is in danger of being submerged in a sea of consumer comforts and luxuries. It would be naive to think that the forward surge of the economy wipes out every economic injustice and puts an end to all economic misery. On the contrary, as an expanding economy showers its gifts on the many, the plight of those who still remain excluded becomes all the more desperate. The relative opulence (for we must use this term for our day by comparison with the days before World War II) of so many in our day gives us no right to ignore the minority that does not even enjoy a decent sufficiency. Indeed, the spreading prosperity makes our continuing inability and lack of determination to resolve the persistent problem of poverty if anything more reprehensible. When all are poor, there is no one to blame, but when only a few are poor, one can blame the rich—or the poor themselves.

Nevertheless, the increasing general prosperity that our economic planners hope to prolong indefinitely, although not a panacea for all social injustice, does take the wind out of the class struggle. West Germany's Christian Democrats have theorized that today the working man must have a share in the ownership of the means of production: he must, in other words, own stock. This they have actively encouraged. In France, former President de Gaulle spoke of "participation," a slogan which also envisions increasing ownership by workers of stock in the industries in which they work. It is not surprising that the leaders of the syndicates (labor unions) and the leftists in general look upon this proposal as an attempt to seduce their adherents. How will they be able to persuade the workers to nationalize a factory in which all the workers own stock?

Certainly the relative and increasing prosperity of whole populations under a moderate system of free enterprise capitalism does not result from the altruism of the capitalists. Prolonged and arduous battles had to be fought by the working classes to rise above the servitude of what was virtual wage-slavery, which lacked even the measure of economic security possessed by many slaves of former times. Great changes lie ahead, and there are battles in the future. But, because the development in the still-free countries did not result in implacable class hatred and did not smash the structure of productivity, there is an increasing production, available to be distributed by a government either of the Right or of the Left, as long as the productive system continues to function and grow.

An inevitable result of this productivity and distribution is the blunting of the class struggle as far as economic classes are concerned. The man who trudged to work through the mud might have come to hate the rich employer who spattered him passing in his carriage. The worker of today who in his Chevrolet or Oldsmobile is jockeying for position in the same congested traffic with his boss in a Cadillac can hardly share a like resentment. The class struggle between different economic levels does not depend merely on the existence of an economic difference: it also depends on the basic level on which the potentially dissatisfied live. A strike for an annual wage increase by people who are already earning five dollars per hour simply cannot carry the same desperate emotional commitment as one made by people who do not earn enough to feed their children.

This inevitable cooling-off of the class struggle with increasing general prosperity confronts those who are committed to the need for a radically changed society with a serious problem. If the working classes become relatively contented and passive, who is going to provide the power to overthrow the existing structures? Where is the necessary force to be drawn from? Who will spark the conflict, and who will wage it, out of which revolutionary progress is to come?

The answer is clear. If the economic classes are insufficiently hostile to each other, new classes must be found. Existing rivalries and injustices must be exacerbated, exaggerated, exploited, and brought to the point of explosion. In short, if economic differences do not provide the necessary tensions, then others must do it. Three have been found, and are beginning to serve well. The new class war is not between economic classes, but between racial groups, age groups, and (a kind of corollary of the second) intellectual groups: between white and black, between young and old, between intellectuals and the vulgar crowd.

4.

Racial Classes

WRITING on the troubled problem of religion and race, seen especially in the light of an atheistic humanist's ardent support of full racial equality and the (South African) Dutch Reformed Church's support for apartheid, Philip Mason states, "I do not think there is any fundamental difference between the animosities that arise between races and those between other groups who are separated by social class, by language or by religion."[1] Is he right in this assertion?

In the United States, with the current color problem and the heritage of Negro slavery, it seems that no animosity could be as bitter as that between races. By a curious and cruel twist of irony, even the Jews, so often the victims of racial hatred and so outstanding in their campaign for Negro rights, have in recent months again experienced the awful impact of racist thinking as many extremist Negroes have begun to engage in a campaign of anti-Semitism as baffling as it is self-destructive and evil. In the Middle East, how-

[1] Philip Mason, *Christianity and Race* (New York: St. Martin's), p. 16.

ever, it is differences of religion, culture, and economic situation, and not of race, which divide the Arabs from the
Jews. Yet so strong is the antipathy of Arabs for Jews that
the illogical expression "Arab anti-Semitism" has become
common. In Northern Ireland, the differences between
Catholics and Protestants are only religious: the racial heritage is the same. In fact, the religious difference did not
become a source of violent hostility between the two segments of Northern Irelands population until it was deliberately exploited for this purpose. Now, however, the
religious antagonism seems as fierce between Protestant and
Catholic Irish as is the racial and cultural antagonism between Punjabis and Bengalis in Pakistan.

A sociologist could certainly devise criteria by which to
distinguish antagonism between different races from that
between different classes. Not least significant is the fact
that while one can pass from class to class with varying degrees of ease, one can hardly pass from race to race. Nevertheless there are basic similarities. For our present discussion,
one similarity is all-important: racial antagonisms can be
used to push an organized, structured society into self-destructive internal struggle in precisely the same way as Marx
envisaged class antagonism doing it. This similarity may be
great enough to allow race war to fulfill the revolutionary
role envisaged by Communist theory for class war. Race
conflict, if unchecked, will destroy the liberal university. It
has gone far towards destroying Harvard and Cornell.

To substitute racial antagonism for antagonism between
economic classes of course plays havoc with the Marxist
theory of progress by class struggle. Perhaps the preoccupation of the consistent Marxist with class struggle is one
reason why the orthodox Communists have been so slow to
profit from racial turmoil in the United States and elsewhere,
despite its obvious potential for disrupting the activities of

a government which is impeding the advance of international communism. Indeed, in view of Communist pronouncements on racial equality, for them deliberately to exacerbate racial tensions and thus to promote racial war would seem hypocritical in the extreme. Nevertheless, in a society such as that of the United States, where genuine economic unrest is at a minimum, a truly chaotic situation of prerevolutionary violence, it appears, can hardly be brought about as old-fashioned class struggle. For this reason the Communists, although belatedly, are stepping into the racial crisis and at the least are deriving some profit from it.

If the "old Left" has qualms about stirring up hatred between races, the New Left does not share them. Motivated by a desire to smash existing structures in the hope that something better will emerge, it does not hesitate to exacerbate existing racial tensions despite the certainty that this will lead to great suffering for all concerned: the ultimate goal is what counts. During the prison riots at Attica, New York, during September, 1971, attorney William Kunstler presented himself as someone who was deeply concerned about the welfare of the rebellious prisoners. Following the successful storming of the prison by state troopers and National Guardsmen, Kunstler was accused by a black on the negotiating committee with having deluded the rebels into believing that the state was under pressure by "Third World" powers and would eventually give in, thus in effect sacrificing the prisoners for the sake of a bloody battle which would radicalize the survivors and many others outside. While some adherents of the "New Left" are simply naive enthusiasts, and others, like "Red Danny" Cohn-Bendit, can easily be seduced by financial gain, it seems hard to deny that others callously produce suicidal confrontations, sacrificing those who trust them for the sake of a long-range goal. Not a pretty posture for those who constantly accuse the United States government of organized hypocrisy!*

In any case, people who suffer from race hatred usually cannot be bought off by improved economic circumstances. In fact, a person who feels himself to be the innocent victim of racial prejudice is apt to feel more strongly about it as his economic situation, his educational attainments, and his level of social achievement all rise. When he was in poverty and ignorance, he may have suspected in spite of himself that the discrimination against him was due to those things. If the discrimination hangs on, though, after he knows full well that he deserves the respect of society, then his bitterness will increase, not decrease, with improvements in his economic and professional situation. A series of interviews with young Negroes enrolled in exclusive preparatory schools reveals the extent to which some of them leave good schools and colleges hopelessly embittered against the existing society and its institutions and armed with the tools to destroy it.[2]

The Permanence of Racial Divisions. The substitution of racial antagonisms for class antagonisms can be partially justified on the grounds that the oppressed race in large measure coincides with the exploited economic class, and that only if it fights as a race—race consciousness being easier to arouse—can it hope quickly to redress the economic balance. This is only partially justified, because while eco-

* I find it hard to believe in the humanitarian zeal of Russian-style Communism, but it must be admitted that in the recent racially-motivated slaughter of Bengalis by Punjabis in East Pakistan, the U.S.S.R., together with India, supported the persecuted Bengalis, while the United States, in company with Red China, gave at least tacit support to the Punjabis from the West.

[2] See Stephen Davenport, "Farewell to the Old School Tie," *Saturday Review*, October 19, 1968, pp. 66ff., and Thee Smith, "I Am the New Black," same issue, p. 68.

nomic differences can be bridged and economic inequities can be overcome, racial differences cannot be. Race hatred cannot be cooled off, once aroused, by economic benefits; its advocates are playing the devil's game. Racial divisions, unlike economic divisions, are more or less constant. There are only two ways to eliminate them: one is a "final solution" like Hitler's; the other is racial amalgamation by rapid interbreeding. As far as a Hitlerian "final solution" is concerned, no sane being worthy of the name human would dream of it, even in nightmares, at least not yet. The reservation "not yet" must be made because *if* the race struggle is substituted for the class struggle, and if it succeeds in overthrowing existing democratic structures with their heritage of Christian ethics and bourgeois morality, it will remain to plague the new order which arises on the ruins of liberal democracy. If such a new order subscribes to the class-struggle, survival-of-the-fittest philosophy, and has preserved none of the restraints of Christianity, a "final solution" will be quite thinkable; one may even say that it will be quite likely.

Today's evolutionary humanists, who seem to have absorbed a dose of what Nietzsche called Christian slave morality, who seem, in other words, to hold onto ethical principles derived from Christianity, would never approve the exploitation of one race by another, not to speak of its suppression (extermination). However, as Mason writes, commenting on Dr. Julian Huxley's mild and humane ethical principles, "It seems to me, if you really follow Dr. Huxley's premises to their logical conclusion, you should say—as Thrasymachus said long ago in Plato's *Republic*— that it is the interest of the stronger that is right. If, therefore, one race has the skill and power to keep another down, it

should do so."[3] If the weaker race represents a constant source
of trouble, who—other than God—has the right to oblige
the stronger to continue to respect its right to live?

The other alternative to the permanence of racial barriers
is intensive interbreeding. This has been proposed by some,
yet it should be quite obvious that, given the geographical
concentration of races by regions, and given the strong
tendency of people to marry within their own racial group,
to hope for a solution by means of racial intermarriage is
very far-fetched. If it were to lead to a noticeable result in
anything less than several millennia, it would not merely have
to be encouraged by governments: it would have to be made
compulsory and universal. What this would involve in
forced transfers of population, in the absolute shattering of
every existing human community and of every family bond
all around the world, staggers the imagination. In order to
be able to bring it to pass, it would be necessary to have a
world authority with absolute and dictatorial powers extending to the most intimate and personal of human decisions.

It is one thing to speak of removing legal, social, and psychological barriers to intermarriage, as a contribution to
reducing racial tensions; but quite another thing indeed
to think that racial intermarriage on a large scale can solve
the problem posed by the existence of differing racial
groups. To bring about the necessary degree of intermarriage
would require absolute and total control of human life and
of the freedom of individual choice. But if such control
existed, it would not be necessary *to require intermarriage*.
Such complete control would be sufficient effectively to forbid every expression of racial animosity. This matrimonial
"cure," although it seems to stand under the sign of love
(or at least of sex) rather than of hatred and cruelty like

[3] Mason, *op. cit.*, p. 18.

Hitler's final solution, would in fact require just as absolute and heartless a dictatorship as Hitler's to accomplish it. It seems reasonable to conclude, then, that racial differences will be with us for a long time—the only way to eliminate them is by a fantastically strong totalitarian tyranny.

Since racial differences are permanent, and since to live in the modern world means that all races are in constant contact with each other, it is evident that we must learn to live with our differences, not dream of destroying or of blending with those who are racially different. This single, obvious fact—the fact that, barring a horrible, inhuman solution, the races of man must live together while maintaining most of their present differences—makes it clear just how *diabolical* (in the service of the diabolos) all racist propaganda and agitation are. Racial tensions, when inflamed, lead to racial violence. And race violence leaves a legacy of hatred which makes the tensions virtually permanent. The involuntary servitude of the Negro in the United States ended over a century ago, but how long will the tensions inherited from that institution continue to blight American history? And what will be the accursed heritage of today's violence and racial crimes, whether they are perpetrated by blacks "to redress the balance" or by whites who "have had enough"?

It is the deliberate exacerbation of racial feeling today which constitutes the most heinous contemporary crime against humanity. It is not only the outright racist agitators, white and black, who are guilty of it. History will show that many prominent and honored political figures of our day, whether moved by subconscious intuition or by deliberate malign cunning, have encouraged Negroes to resentment and violence in the hopes of frightening the general public into electing them to office. Then they would hope to solve the problems that they themselves had exacerbated. This is rather like Hitler sending German troops in Polish uniforms to attack a German radio station, the pretext for the German invasion of Poland. Others have wagered on the opposite horse, fanning the smouldering flames of white resentment in the expectation that they could thereby rise to power. Today we accuse the little demagogues, the petty white racists and the Black Power people, of being responsible for race hatred. But history will some day recognize that many men in high places, whose personal conduct is characterized by urbanity and tolerance, have in fact done more to produce and to aggravate the racial tensions than the resentful little men.

The situation in Western countries that have a domestic race problem, such as the United States and even Great Britain, has not yet reached the point of desperate, internecine violence, as in Pakistan and the Sudan. But the already-existing animosity, fanned by calculating politicians and by the unreflected reactions of those who bear the scars of past injustice and present arrogance, is a powder keg. It could explode into destructive violence at any moment. The violence that could erupt in Britain would hardly destroy that country; there the minority race is not numerous enough to topple the society. But it could destroy every vestige of decency, democracy, and of humane civilization which remains there. In the United States likewise a violent and prolonged racial struggle could not, in all probability, destroy the established order, which has considerable resiliency and great power at its disposal. However, the functioning of the democratic machinery could be rendered impossible, so that a dictatorship would emerge as the only alternative to perpetual chaos. It goes without saying that there are foreign powers that would certainly not disdain the opportunity to profit from severe internal struggles in the United States. Perhaps these powers abstain from promoting race conflict to the full extent of their ability because they have reason to dread the military dictatorship which might arise out of it more than the present bourgeois democracy.

Racist thinking is certainly one of the most pernicious factors in any society. It is also one of the most pervasive. Because it is so pervasive, because it lies so close to the surface in every society, there is always a temptation to make use of it to accomplish political or social ends. There are two deep reasons why racist thinking so easily can be aroused and stimulated and why, once it is aroused, it is so difficult to eradicate.

The Gregarious Nature of Man. This is a fundamental psychological reality. Few indeed are those who can live as a wolf of the steppes (to use Hermann Hesse's word for the man who is an extreme and consistent individualist). The Dutch philosopher, Professor Herman Dooyeweerd, has pointed out that the human self is empty until it takes on content by relating to other selves, a fact so obivous as to require no further demonstration. This gregarious nature means that we tend to congregate in groups to which we are attached or attracted, and to derive much of our emotional security from the identification with them. Sometimes the bond which creates a strong group feeling is acquired by deliberate choice, as when one joins a religious fellowship or a political action group. More often it is determined by factors such as a common language, closeness in age, etc. The gregarious impulse has positive value, in that it builds a community of spirit. It has a negative aspect in that it naturally excludes from its fellowship those who do not share the common bond; from exclusion it is but a step to dislike, discrimination, and real animosity. To recognize this is not to speak against communities, clubs, and cliques, for they are natural and necessary; it is merely to recognize that they can also occasion trouble.

Racial similarities are among the most obvious characteristics which can be used to form a bond between people who are alike and to exclude those who are different. Racial differences can pose a problem only when different races live together in close proximity. So strong is the human tendency to form exclusive groups, however, that it often happens that where real racial differences do not exist, even minor distinctions of appearance or speech produce racist feelings which can persist for centuries. When the differences are great, as between Caucasians and Negroes, it is impossible to avoid a *consciousness* of the fact that such differences exist. This consciousness need not produce racist feelings of contempt and animosity. It can be overcome if members of the different races are united by shared convictions, by common interests, or by personal ties of another kind. The armed forces of many nations have successfully overcome racial differences.

All of these mitigating factors, which can conquer racial animosity and build a sense of community that transcends race, have a personal dimension. They depend on people being able to respond to others as individuals, as persons. True racist thinking, by contrast, depends on people thinking and reacting *en bloc*. When people do begin to react *en bloc*, then previously important personal ties simply melt away. Because of the power which individual ties can have in people who possess a certain strength of character, racist propaganda naturally seeks to destroy all such interracial relationships. "He is my friend," receives the response, "It makes no difference; he's white [or black, or a Jew, or a German, etc., etc.]." Strong communities that exist and transcend racial differences will be attacked as well. Hence Black Power, for example, attacks communities as different as Christian churches and Olympic teams. Men and women of different races must not be allowed to feel that they have *anything* important and psychologically valuable in common.

The stronger an individual is in his own sense of personal identity and personal assurance, the less likely he will be to let racist or other bloc-thinking override his personal loyalties to other individuals. The insecure individual, however, is easily shaken. In our age the forces that give an individual a strong sense of personal value and responsibility, chief among them the force of personal religious faith, have been drastically weakened. In consequence, the weakened, insecure individual, incapable of being "inner-directed" by a strong inward conviction and sense of purpose, easily falls prey to racism, which gives him a sense of identity he otherwise lacks.

Racism, if it is to advance, depends on preventing people from thinking and feeling as true individuals. It must destroy, for example, orthodox Christian faith, for Christianity gives an individual a strong consciousness of his personal dignity and personal responsibility before a personal God, a consciousness based on grace, not race. This explains the fact that although Christianity has seldom been expressly or strongly antiracist, all racist movements have shown a strong hostility to the Christian faith. Hitler feared and Black Power extremists still fear the "weakening" effect of Christian faith on those they are trying to influence.* It also explains why racism is self-perpetuating:

* One significant exception is South Africa, where the Christian church (at least the Dutch Reformed Church) supports apartheid. Does this suggest that there are significant differences between the thinking behind South African apartheid and that of German or American racism? As a Christian and a Calvinist who is deeply troubled by apartheid and by Calvinistic support for it, I must hope that some such differences may exist, that is, that all the talk of the white South Africans about desiring

it destroys individuality, and those whose individuality has once been destroyed continue to need the herd-like support of racism and can escape its influence only with the greatest difficulty. If Christian or national identity has been lost, only racial identity remains.

Racism Is Diabolical in Inspiration. If the gregarious tendency, which is innate in man and which can easily be perverted into racist thinking, is the first cause for the prevalence of racism, the second is plainly enough its diabolical background. In our late twentieth-century culture we find it embarrassing to speak of the devil and of *his* role in our history.[4] But if we do not wish to see any *satanic* influence in Nazism, for example, to whom can we ascribe its depths of evil? One answer would be that Nazi racism *was due to man as man.* But consider the implications of such a statement!

This answer fits the behavior of other men elsewhere, for Nazism is not altogether unique. Taken seriously, it would lead man to despair of himself. Taken seriously, it also shows man his need for redemption. But most modern men do not want to begin thinking along lines that could lead them into a dilemma from which only God could rescue them, nor is it likely that the devil would want to push them into one. Thus the alternative answer is given: Nazism came out of the heart of *Germans*, not out of the heart of *man.* This in turn leads back to the illusion that evil can be overcome by destroying a certain "class," in this case, a nation or race, which we have defined as the source of all evil. This is nothing less than racism perpetuating

to help the Bantu develop in an integral way contains a germ of truth. It cannot be proved, but perhaps it is there. Nevertheless, it is not enough to permit a non–South African Christian to do other than oppose the present policies of that country's government.

[4] Denis de Rougemont was courageous enough to dedicate a whole book to this topic, *La part du diable* (Neuchâtel: La Baconnière, 1945), *The Devil's Share* (New York: Pantheon, 1945).

itself; Nazism can thus survive with a new name and with new spokesmen, though all the Nazis be killed, and the work of the *diabolos* can go forward. If Nazi racism is purely German, then men are divided once again from each other; then human solidarity vanishes again, and with it individual responsibility. Is it not always easier and more desirable to combat evil outside oneself, as incorporated in a particular race, by hating that race's members, than to have to combat it within one's heart, by turning to God and denying oneself? How strange that American society rushes to take the blame for small-scale crimes like political assassinations, but attributes the big ones to another race!

According to biblical teaching, it is the individual who is responsible (answerable) to God. Human solidarity exists, and racial solidarity exists as well. Nevertheless, it is as an individual that each man lives and dies and as an individual that he will stand before the judgment seat of God (II CORINTHIANS 5:10). The Christian faith promises to each individual a personal destiny, a destiny which depends on his own particular response to God in this life. This great emphasis on personal responsibility and on eternity has often caused the church to take a quietistic, passive attitude towards social injustice in the world and has sometimes led Christians to reject their responsibilities as members of the society in which they live. This can and should be admitted, condemned, and counteracted, but it must not be counteracted by substituting racist thought. The humanistic "white liberals" of the 1940's and 1950's, whose ideal was for people to be color-blind, were also shortsighted: they could not recognize the degree to which the form of gregariousness rooted in race is natural to man; not believing in the devil, they could not imagine that there was any power evil enough to try to turn this innate tend-

ency into a raging force able to fragment mankind and
to destroy human individuality.

Now we know better. We can see the evil face of the
giant called Black Power, roused from a long sleep of
slavery and servitude by the continuing oppression of white
men. We can also see a recrudescent White Power taking
its excuse if not its real origin from the excesses of Black
Power, which could all too easily sweep away the weak
restraints of optimistic, humanistic charity and inaugurate
a new era of scientific barbarism. The liberals of the forties
and fifties did not foresee this. How could they, believing
in the natural goodness of man and denying the devil?

What is the solution? There is only one: to recognize
the diabolical nature of all attempts to divide men along
racial lines. We must renounce and condemn *every* attempt
to do so, regardless of what benevolent long-range goal it
may seem to serve. We must recognize that human solidarity before God is *as mankind,* not as a particular race, and
that human responsibility to Him must be faced by men
as individuals.

At its Fourth Assembly in Uppsala, Sweden (July 1968),
the World Council of Churches was quite frank in its condemnation of this evil: "Especially we shall seek to overcome racism wherever it appears."[5] Whether the WCC

[5] From "The Message of the Assembly," printed in Kenneth Strack,
Uppsala Report (London: S.C.M., 1968), p. vii. Since 1968 the W.C.C.
has appropriated $400,000, some of it from money originally intended for
evangelism and world mission, for "liberation" movements in various countries, but chiefly in southern Africa. Unless my figures are in error, this is
the first W.C.C. project to receive more than token support from behind
the Iron Curtain (over $400,000 promised by the Evangelical Church of
the so-called German Democratic Republic alone). In view of the fact
that substantial portions of this money have gone directly to organizations
engaged in anti-white terrorism, I leave it to the reader to judge the precise
meaning of the W.C.C.'s determination to "overcome racism wherever it
appears." Or do we accept the new convention which holds that only
whites can be racists, and that anything which might seem like race hatred
on the part of another group is always "understandable" is not actually
praiseworthy?

Assembly's positive pronouncements were all that might have been expected of a Christian organization with roots in the old International Missionary Council, at least it saw quite clearly in singling out the one significant evil of racism for condemnation. Even if racism is in theory fundamentally no different from other forms of class pride and arrogance, its potential for evil is so great and its baneful influence is so long-lasting that it must be given first place among contemporary social evils which the church should combat. The WCC knows this. But how does it know it? There is not much use in denouncing an evil unless you can persuade people to renounce it by so doing. What is lacking in most church pronouncements against racism (and many other evils) is a clear statement of the will of God and of His sanctions against sin.

Over and beyond the failure to give an adequate reason for its condemnation, the error of the WCC and of contemporary Christianity generally, in dealing not only with the question of race but also with other social issues, lies in not taking seriously the priority stated by Jesus, "Seek ye first the Kingdom of God and His righteousness" (MATTHEW 6:33). In the final analysis, who is to forbid a particular race, which through accident or effort is in a dominant position, to assume itself to be superior and to seek to keep all the other races in a position of inferiority? The only valid answer is that the righteousness of God forbids it. Evolutionary ethics, pace Dr. Huxley, can easily be read to approve the subjugation by the "preferred races" of the less preferred, just as most liberal intellectuals advocate the dominance of an intellectual elite over the boorish masses.

During the period of European and American imperialistic expansion, the white races of Europe and America certainly acted in a naively racist manner. Their technical

superiority used to permit them to dominate or at least
to intimidate the world's other racial families, and they
did not have many qualms about it. Eventually, however,
under the contemporaneous if mutually opposed nine-
teenth-century influences of the evangelistic and missionary
flowering on the one hand and of the rise of optimistic,
evolution-oriented liberalism on the other, they were being
prepared to give up their naive racist pretensions and to
stop *acting* like a master race (even though many Caucasians continue to think like one). Today the former
colonial powers of both Europe and the United States have
voluntarily withdrawn from positions of dominance over
other races from which they could hardly have been
driven by force if they really had been thinking in racist
terms. It is one of the ironies of history that racist prejudices, both native and transplanted, are now stirring up
formerly subject races to perpetrate the same crimes under
which they themselves suffered. They are even ready to
perpetrate them in a more dreadful manner than their
former European oppressors, whose excesses were at least
sometimes tempered by Christian or democratic sentiments.

A great hue and cry is constantly being raised against
the growing isolation of individuals and the loss of true
communities in our urbanized, technological civilization.
The tendencies to mass action (student protests in
Berkeley, New York, Paris, Berlin, and Rome) are often
presented as protests against the increasing depersonali-
zation which characterizes our society. There is some
validity in this, yet participation in such mass actions may
have exactly the opposite effect. It may destroy the vestiges
of individuality which still exist in the individual and
which still are tolerated by the state. As part of a mass,
a student can easily bring himself to do something he

would never do acting singly; in a mob, personal responsibility disappears. Confronted with mass disorders, a government sees itself faced with the choice between repressive
violence and surrender. A weak government will be destroyed; a strong government will hold out, but only by
determining the crush the freedom which its citizens are
turning into chaos.

This again reemphasizes the essentially diabolic nature
of racist thought. An unruly crowd that becomes a wild
mob because of economic resentment may be shocked back
into sanity at the thought of what its violence may do to
its own goods. The reasons why the French riots of May–
June 1968 sputtered out without wrecking the government
certainly included the fact that so many of the French
workers finally realized that they were injuring themselves
economically. Racial resentments do not so easily succumb
to such considerations. Race hatred, when it has erupted
into violence, aims at destroying people, not only goods
and property; once a great quantity of blood has been shed
in civil strife, sanity seldom returns except at the point
of a tyrant's sword.

The responsibility of the Christian, then, is absolute
opposition to all forms of racist thinking. This opposition
must not be in the name of a feigned evolutionary solidarity of mankind, for that argument can cut two ways. It
must be in the name of a particular kind of *individualism*,
a complete, absolute, and atomistic individualism, if you
will, one which destroys any hope that a man might have
of shucking his responsibility onto a group. It is the
individualism based on an awareness of each man's personal
answerability to the divine Judge. This opposition to racist
thinking will also be in the name of a *human solidarity*
of the most complete, absolute, and universal kind, a
solidarity which destroys the claim of any race to a special

position above others. It is the solidarity of all men, all in like manner created by God, all in like manner in rebellion against Him, and all in like manner offered the gift of sonship through the Son of God, who became not a Son of Israel or of any other race, but the Son of Man.

To take the political phenomenon of racism seriously means to recognize that it is quite capable of destroying civilization and of crushing democracy and freedom. To take the reality of Christ seriously means that we must fight racism *in His name*, for in Him and *only* in Him, are we all children of one Father; outside Him we become the hateful and hating victims of the Divider, cut off from one another and from God.

5.

The Races of Young and Old

THE Reverend Eric Fife, an Englishman who for many years worked with the Inter-Varsity Christian Fellowship among college and university students in America, used to say when asked to introduce himself, "I am a missionary working among the unevangelized tribes of the North American campus." Fife's words were not meant as a joke, even a decade ago. In the United States, that most self-consciously Christian among nominal Christian nations, most of the members of recent college generations have reached manhood with a "liberal education," but without any idea of what the Christian Gospel really says. Dr. William G. Pollard, the director of the Oak Ridge Atomic Laboratories who became an Episcopal minister, has pointed out that a three-year-old knows about television and how to turn it on, but that adults in our "Christian" society have no idea what is meant by the forgiveness of God, nor how to obtain it.[1] Dr. Francis A. Schaeffer, a noted American theologian and critic of contemporary thought living in Switzerland, believes that "modern man"

[1] See his essay, "Dark Age and Renaissance in the Twentieth Century," *The Christian Idea of Education*, ed. Edmund Fuller (New Haven: Yale, 1957), pp. 1–22.

is so indoctrinated with relativism and so inoculated against the possibility that something is really true that he cannot even understand what the Christian message says, much less conceive of what it might mean to him.[2]

If the student generation of ten years ago was aptly termed unevangelized there was possibly something whimsical in Fife's references to it as consisting of "tribes." Today there is nothing whimsical about the designation. The kind of tribalization projected by our hippies has not yet progressed very far: all their tribes have not yet gathered. But "tribal thinking" is sweeping back over the city culture of the world, and the student generation is becoming rapidly tribalized.

Civilization, in both classical and medieval times, was almost exclusively associated with and produced by city and town culture. It is only in our century that city-dwellers have become numerically dominant, but long before it was city-building that spelled the difference between civilization, which orders human life, and the rude chaos of barbarism. It was in town and city life that free institutions developed, that specialization flourished, that different trades and professions met and interacted. Thus an ordered complexity, diversity, and freedom came into the conditions of human life. The university too was itself a kind of city (although historically not all important universities were founded *in* large towns or cities). The *universitas magistrorum at scholarum*, the totality of teachers and students, from which our word "university" comes, brought intellectual order out of diversity.

But if the town, the city, and the university used to provide a structure, an order, and thus a protective environment for diversity, the opposite is true today. It is in the city and in the university that such diversity now comes

2 Francis A. Schaeffer, *The God Who Is There* (London: Hodder and Stoughton; Chicago: Inter-Varsity, 1968), esp. pp. 119ff.

under greatest pressure. The urban university is the most hostile environment of all. The university, no longer a stronghold of intellectual diversity, today is at the forefront of the retribalization of civilization. The law, the customs, the distinctions of civilization with its specialization and diversities fade, and only the tribe, a primitive community without institutions but under a central and powerful authority, remains. Thus far we have spoken only of students as "tribes." But since in most countries only a small fraction of those of college age ever go to a university, it will be more useful to speak not merely of the tribes who are at universities, but of the race to which they belong, the race whose members are short-lived but which is always being replenished: the young.

If the devil's share in our society, to use de Rougemont's term, is indicated by his success as the Divider, that share is great and it is growing. In only one area have Western societies been overcoming the fragmentation of humanity in which the diabolos rejoices: in economics. There, as we know, the old Marxist hope that constantly mounting tensions would lead to class war has faded. But the diabolos has developed a whole new realm of tensions, more easily inflamed, more persistent, and potentially productive of great hatred. The class war of today is race war; the classes of today are races.

Yet not every society includes different races; most European nations have no grave racial tensions. And race hatred *might* just burn itself out in a destructive race war with a "final solution." The devil would not be the devil if he did not have a problem in reserve. Even as antagonisms between races, in the usual sense of the word, mount, a new kind of "race" is appearing. Today's new classes are the races, and the new races of today are the generations. The new race war, which has already begun to make its appearance even before all the old-style racial animosities have fully come to a head, is war between the generations. Generation or "age war," already beginning to glow like burning cities on the horizon of our future, is a new triumph of the Divider. Perhaps it will be his deadliest, for it is perpetual and self-perpetuating.

THE SWORD OF THE GENERATIONS

Racism, though capable of destroying a society or a community, at least preserves the elementary bonds between parents and children, between brother and brother. The sword that is used in the generation conflict, which is becoming an age war, divides father from son, even brother from brother. A ten-year gap is not unusual between brothers, and it is enough. The "oppressed" instigators of this new class war, the "revolting masses," the young students, teenagers, and alienated young adults, do not recognize it yet, but the sword of the generation war, which they are whetting, if not quickly broken, will cut into their own flesh as well. It will not merely cut them off from their own children, as they have been cut from their parents, but it will cut them off from themselves, from what they have been and what they will be. The age war, from the nature of things, will not be as bloody as the race war. The son may think that his father treats him as a slave, yet even abused Negro slaves were reluctant to kill their white masters; apart from the fury of tragedy, even the most alienated son will hardly shed his father's blood. Nevertheless, the conflict will be alienating and deeply tragic. The sword with which one generation frees itself from the past will bite deep into its own body, for after the passage of a few years, the young are no longer so young, and the weapons of disdain and alienation which they wielded against their elders will be turned all the more cruelly against them. To permit (not to say to encourage) drastic antagonism for their elders because they are older is self-destructive folly on the part of the young.

The conflict between the generations is as old as mankind, although the first murder (following Genesis and not Freud) was fratricide, not patricide. After Cain's murder of Abel, the Bible and other ancient documents are full of reports which reflect conflicts between the generations: the tragic story of Absalom's rebellion against David is but one example. Homer's *Iliad* tells us of Hector's noble filial love for Priam, but the disaster that came upon Troy was the result of the rebellion of another son of Priam's, Paris, against his father's authority represented by the code of his society. There are enough examples in the history of literature to make it quite clear that the generation gap is nothing new. Yet today it is deeper and more embittered than at any other era in human history. From being a transitory problem through which every family passes, just as the individual passes through puberty, it is becoming a chronic, self-perpetuating condition. It has been elevated to a principle, a principle according to which many claim the whole of society must be remade. It is an incoherent principle, because youth is a passing stage. One can listen to youths, but not to "youth." Youth is not a principle or a system that can be adopted and followed. Those whom a revolution in favor of youth would favor with power today would be cast out tomorrow. But having had power, would a successfully rebellious youthful generation of today softly hand it over to tomorrow's young? To do so would be to admit that they had passed over into the class they rejected and despised.

An important principle is at stake here. To admit that only a certain age group can have the necessary mental ability to rule (be it the young or the old) is to say that thought and all the creative products of the human mind are *biological* phenomena. It is to imply that the observations, judgments, and creative work that come from the mind of a man have no intrinsic value in themselves, but are to be evaluated in terms of the age of the man making them. We do not even deny to an insane man the possibility of saying valuable and true things. Nietzsche, for example, wrote his later works after his mind had been seriously affected, but we take them seriously nonetheless. Yet to take the implicit principle of the generation gap seriously would be to say that what the old (or the young) say is to be disqualified because they are old (or young). It is not likely that a generation which accepted this principle when young, and gained power thereby, would abide by it when old, and willingly surrender its power.

We must admit that making the generation gap—or to put it more positively, youth power or student power— into a principle is a self-defeating kind of procedure, for today's young rather quickly become tomorrow's middle-aged, and if they are able to bluff today's middle-aged into giving *them* power, later they probably will not be so easily bluffed by today's small children, their juniors. Nevertheless, if it is an unsound principle, it is a widely espoused and acclaimed one. Why do the young so deeply feel the need for power that it has become a kind of an obsession among many of them? Why is there, among the no-longer-young, a kind of paralysis of the will? Why is there the general revolt against authority on the one hand, and the abdication of its exercise on the other? To answer these questions with the fulness they merit would take us far beyond the limits of this work. It will be necessary to confine ourselves to mentioning only the main factors involved. One factor may be called ideological, or perhaps religious; the other, psychological or educational.

The Loss of a Sense of Personal and of Human Destiny.
Darwin, Marx, and Freud, those three great figures of nine-
teenth-century and early twentieth-century thought, have
brought our civilization to a loss of a sense of individual
destiny and national or racial (human) purpose. With his
doctrine of the evolutionary origin of *Homo sapiens*, Darwin
undermined man's confidence in himself as having a special
place in God's created order; Marx, with his materialistic
historical determinism, discredited the hope that history has
transcendent meaning or fulfills a divine plan; by his psychological determinism, Freud destroyed for many people the
sense of the meaningfulness of moral choices and of personal responsibility. We should add the name of Nietzsche,
whose talk of the death of God became fashionable in
the last decade. The net impact of this kind of thought,
popularized and widely accepted, followed by the terrible
shocks of World War I, the economic crisis of the interwar
years, and World War II, destroyed the optimistic faith in
progress which characterized the late nineteenth and early
twentieth century. Men began to think of themselves as no
more than slightly rational monkeys, more handicapped
than helped by their intelligence. Economic and psychological determinism convinced millions that meaningful
personal choices are impossible. All this produced a sense
of paralysis of the will more severe than that which results
from the worst exaggerations of the Christian doctrine of
predestination. The predestinarian emphasizes above all
the sovereign will of God,[3] and this might theoretically

[3] The Christian doctrine of predestination is more complex and less fatal
to human freedom and responsibility than is generally supposed. Rather
than attempt to discuss it, let us heed Calvin's warning, "When they
inquire into predestination, they penetrate the inmost recesses of Divine
wisdom, where the careless and confident intruder will obtain no satisfaction for his curiosity, but will enter a labyrinth from which he will find
no possibility to depart" (*Institutes of the Christian Religion*, Book III,
Ch. 1:1).

cripple his own will, but he has the great consolation that it is a loving and wise God who predestines, and can follow Calvin's advice to believe that he is predestined to glory and to pattern his life accordingly. The determinism of Darwin, Marx, and Freud is that of blind, inflexible, impersonal laws, which know neither justice nor mercy. Even the most severe Puritan would never have dreamed of failing to ascribe mercy to God. It is interesting that Calvinists often exhibit considerable willpower: apparently a doctrine of divine predestination does not inhibit it!

The nineteenth century was a time of liberalism in theology. This meant that the concepts of a personal Judge and of a divine Savior were abandoned, together with that of a believable and authoritative revelation. The definite doctrines of the creeds and Reformation confessions were replaced in religious circles by a vague kind of faith in the universal fatherhood of God; in secularly minded circles they were superseded entirely.[4] Perhaps the crucial factor in this change of outlook was the loss of any sense of an *intelligible divine plan* or law. Both Darwin and Marx retained, in an inconsistent way, a kind of a sense of destiny and of the goodness of progress, but it was a destiny deprived of all meaning, for there was no standard by which to call "progress" good. "Destiny" still ruled, but the *logos* had gone out of it. Without any divine, creative Word, by whom all things were made and held together (JOHN 1:3, HEBREWS 1:3), there is no reason to call a man better than an amoeba or a city more valuable than an ant heap. In biblical thought the divine Word has many characteristics that far transcend human knowing and remain mysteries to us, but it also can, in part at

---

[4] See Karl Barth, *From Rousseau to Ritschl* (London: S.C.M., 1959), and Colin Brown, *Philosophy and the Christian Faith* (London: Tyndale, 1969).

least, be spoken *in human language*, and that which is spoken can be understood. It is not totally incomprehensible, and therefore life ceases to be what the pagan Aeschylus called it, "bewildering mystery."

The law of God seems hard to man: it sets a standard to which he is both unwilling and unable to adhere. It is a *knowable* standard, and this is crucial. The old determinism was an absolute monarchy, if you will, but the Monarch *spoke the language of his subjects* and told them that He would be a Father to them. The new determinism, the "laws" of evolution, dialectical materialism, etc., are not only blind, but mute. They do not speak a strange and difficult language like the Hebrew and Greek of the Bible, but no language at all. With the loss of the intelligible word about a personally directing Providence comes a subjugation to blind, impersonal process.

The old, Christian view of nature as the planned and good Creation of an all-wise God taught that the elements of order in nature, the "laws of nature," were impressed upon it by the same creative Word which expressed itself in verbal form in the revelation recorded in the Bible. The man reading the Word of God in Scripture was in a real sense in tune with the universe and its Author. In such an ordered universe, with both physical and moral laws operating, it was natural to have an order in human society; the social structure was seen as a necessary and valid reflection of the greater divinely established order of the universe.

There may have been a certain arrogance involved in the assumption of the rulers of an earlier era that their rule somehow represented the order established by God. On the other hand, there is something terribly pathetic in the rulers and officials of the Western world today, who seem to lack the confidence that they represent anyone or anything more important than themselves. In place of the arrogant rulers and haughty magistrates of an earlier day, elected and appointed officials today seem apologetic, fearful, completely lacking in self-respect and in a sense of the dignity and responsibility of office. As a result, they are unable to assert themselves and their principles in the face of a determined challenge even from a small minority. The spectacle of policemen and National Guardsmen watching in confusion while stores were looted before their eyes— a spectacle seen all across America on nationwide television —was pathetic, but the really weak and pitiable figures were the officials giving the orders, who lacked the will to fulfill their sworn obligations. If the mandate to govern involves a duty as well as a privilege, then the abdication by many governors of their governing authority constitutes an abandonment of responsibility. The most tragic thing about the refusal of the older generation to exercise the authority with which it has been entrusted, thinking that its refusal serves the cause of freedom, is that such failure will ultimately make freedom itself impossible. To surrender the prerogatives of age when faced with the impetuosity of youth is, in the last analysis, to deny the intellectual value of human civilization and to assert the supremacy of the merely biological in human life. This is consistent with the evolutionary principle of struggle discussed earlier, but it does not leave much room for either a Christian or a humanist view of the dignity of man. It deprives youth of its *human* heritage and leaves it mere animal vigor.

Renunciation of the Future. In other words, the young can assert their preeminence only at the expense of the old, who represent what they themselves will become. The implicit claim to dominance by those on the threshold of biological maturity involves a turning away from their own future. The young who merely demand to be allowed to participate in shaping *their own future* are reasonable, but when they demand that they, as today's youth, shape the future as such, they go too far, for in the world of tomorrow in which they will live, they will be the old and no longer free, but subject to today's infants. To be "the Now generation" is to abandon tomorrow. Perhaps tomorrow's old people will prove less complaisant than today's and will not turn over to their juniors the power they have wrested from their seniors. If instead our young people remain consistent, and should let today's infants rule them in tomorrow's world, they would thereby close the door to their own future and prepare for themselves an era of subjugation and degradation.

It is in fact not likely that many of the agitators for "youth power" reflect much on the day, not so far distant, when they will be its victims, not its beneficiaries. Nevertheless, they should do it. Those who refuse may thereby strengthen their claim to the title "the Now generation," but they also demonstrate that they lack one of the primary qualities of civilized man: an awareness of time. Without a sense of time, civilization is impossible, and so is purpose. Life becomes a dream. The lack of an awareness of time is also responsible for another major characteristic of the gathering age war: the repudiation of the past. What people fail to see is that to repudiate the past is to renounce the future.

The Repudiation of the Past. There is a sense in which today is all we actually ever have. The past is forever gone and tomorrow never comes. Yet it is precisely the characteristic of primitive man as opposed to civilized man that he has no real sense of his own past, nor of his own future. He has myths and legends, but no history. In our aspirations and plans, the future is already with us; in our traditions and institutions, the past continues to live on. There is a sense in which man can become a prisoner of his future, or of his past. Preoccupation with a future life in heaven may conceivably paralyze some people for the present life on earth. The same is true in a sense for the Communist dream. The modern forms of mass servitude known as communism in all its many varieties make the men of today the slaves of those of tomorrow. The hope of communism is that the men of tomorrow will be happy, and will not be the slaves of the day after tomorrow as those of today are theirs, and so on *ad infinitum*.

Bondage to the past comes when the traditions and institutions dominate completely, when they destroy the ability of man today to discover, to experience, to plan, to work and to create for himself, and force him into preset patterns. This bondage can become outright slavery if the preset patterns are too incompatible with the actual conditions of today's world, and force men to work without understanding why and deny them the results of their labors. The tradition of pyramid-building made many slaves; other traditions can do as much today.

Although it is true that such bondage can exist, it is also true that without the past there is no future, and the present loses its intellectual content and becomes meaningless. Specifically, without the past, one cuts oneself off from one's own kind, from all the hopes and aspirations of those who have gone before, and of which we in the present are the bearers. Dead tradition is deadening, but living traditions strengthen life, not weaken it. The revolt of the young against the old *as old* is a revolt against the very existence of tradition (*traditio*, what is handed down) as well as against those who are handing it down. There are some who argue that many young rebels unconsciously hope that the tradition will reassert itself. In other words, they are like disobedient children who have lost their sense of order and oughtness and want to provoke their parents into re-establishing it. That may be true, but if it is, they will be disappointed. In almost every case the bearers of tradition in today's world are in headlong retreat.

To revolt against a particular tradition because it is thought harmful or bad is one thing; to revolt against all tradition simply because it is *handed down* is quite another. Slavery was a tradition, as was racial discrimination; the revolts against them were morally justified. It was not the fact that they were *traditional* that made them wrong, but rather that their content was wrong. A tradition that teaches that human servitude is good is wrong because human servitude is wrong, not because it is a tradition. That it is a tradition simply means that it is communicated to us by our predecessors; it would be just as wrong if it had just been invented for the first time in the history of the world. And let there be no doubt about it: the radicals of the New Left, given the necessary power, would invent some things of their own, and "hand them down" in quite an obligatory way to all those with the misfortune to be subject to them.

An Exaltation of Tradition? To say that human tradition cannot err would be tantamount to saying that man is capable of avoiding all error, which is manifestly false. To say, on the other hand, that what is traditional is wrong and that only what is new is valid is to say that man always errs; and that, fundamentally, is to say that even the most recent human action and human thought are meaningless or will shortly be so. To be more precise, to condemn tradition as tradition could be to say, since tradition expresses a *consensus* of the past, that the majority is always wrong. There is an elitism implicit in this that leads to tyranny.

Alternatively, since the consensus is in the *past*, it might say that the wheel of progress turns so rapidly that only the present instant is valid and that all that is past is not even prologue, but just noise. The inescapable conclusion from the elitist rejection of tradition as *the voice of a consensus* is that the self-appointed "knowledgeable minority" has the right to dominate the majority, even against its will. The conclusion from the rejection of tradition as *the voice of the past*, as *heritage*, is that only the *now* is authoritative, and that in turn is to reject all memory and meaning, all gathered, ordered science, in favor of a spontaneous, momentary intuition. It has often been noticed that very few students of the natural sciences or of medicine are in the radical movements. One reason must be the fact that their kind of science is so much more immediate and tangible than that of philosophy, sociology, or what passes for theology, that they *know* it is real. The mature scientist knows that science is not everything, but he also knows that it is *something*. Thus he cannot discard the whole of tradition, for tradition provided him with the tools and methods to deal with something that is real.

Of course, no one does consistently and thoroughly reject all tradition, simply because tradition, in one real sense, gives us everything we have, right down to the very languages we must use to communicate with each other. The violent attacks on traditional institutions and values are themselves traditional and are based on a different set of values handed down by different people. Truly to break with the past, each man would have to have his own language, or else to say nothing at all. Of course this is not possible for the protesters; it would be self-defeating. Even so, the tendency to praise the ineffable, unutterable, drug-induced experience which takes place in a private world with no communication possible, is an attempt in the direction of no language, no words at all. It is a radical consequence of antitraditionalism. Its ultimate consequence would be a world of atomistic individuals, forever isolated, each lost in the perpetual contemplation of his own private world. Those who dream of such a situation should reflect that an anarchistic revolution is hardly likely to establish any such atomistic freedom, but rather its opposite—the collectivity of a dictatorship. The ultimate effect of such thinking is to say that the analytical, theoretical intellect of man is worthless, and that all that is important is the spark of spontaneity. Again, life is reduced to mere biology. The catch is that the anarchists really do not want life as mere biology: for many of them, as for Daniel Cohn-Bendit, now launched in writing and moviemaking (and money-making), anarchy is a pretense to get the current "ins" out so that they can get themselves in. Thus the whole movement of radical protest has a certain fraudulent quality about it. Nevertheless, it is serious, and dangerous, because the power of chaos is real.

In the eyes of many people, it is spontaneity itself which is intellectual, creative, form-giving. Admittedly, a spark of intuition can add something to a situation that was not there at all before. But how can we recognize that something is creative, that it is new, unless the forms of the past are there with which it can be compared? Cut off from the substance of an intellectual tradition, the creative spark just flies up and dies like fireworks in a night sky: there is nothing for it to ignite.

Ultimately, then, spontaneity results in an assertion of the merely *biological* over the noetic (from Greek *nous*, mind), the intellectual. Only that is spontaneous which does not reflect upon the past or plan for the future. But spontaneity in this sense is only preintellectual, *merely* biological life. The generation war, then, as a principle, means the assertion of the *bios* over the *nous*, of the blood over the mind.

The Age of Reason, because it ascribed to the *nous* an uncontested rule which it never had possessed since the Fall of Man, and the following period of Idealism, can be accused of having given Mind a sovereignty in the life of man which was not its due. Man is not just a reason that chances to inhabit a physical body. Many, many persistent errors stem from this false sovereignty of the reason, not least among them the widespread assumption of "liberal" political thought that evil is based on ignorance and can be cured by education and a better environment (by feeding the reason). The Christian faith is absolutely opposed to this: for the most evil and rebellious of all creatures, the devil, is among the most intelligent and best informed. Forgetting this, many Christians fell under the spell of the Enlightenment and of Idealism, and forgot man's *bios*, his animal life. It is only recently that they have begun to escape their baleful influence.

Sigmund Freud startled the world with his revelation of the small part the conscious mind (the reason), with its ability to reflect and to analyze, plays in the life of man. Rivals and opponents were quick to correct him and to gainsay him on many points, and his understanding of what man really is, if fully accepted, will cause more problems than it solves. Nevertheless, after Freud, it will never again be possible for us to look upon man as essentially only a reasoning mind that incidentally happens to dwell in a body of flesh and blood.

If the Age of Reason induced a false optimism and thus paved the way for the shock and despair which have swept over much of the world as man's darker passions reasserted themselves, the dawning Age of Unreason is placing the *nous* in complete subjection.

TIME AND HUMAN FREEDOM

The University as the Battlefield. Perhaps no other institution in the Western world, except the church, is as conscious of tradition and as much a bearer of tradition as is the university. Even France, a country which has gone through two empires, two monarchies, and is now in its Fifth Republic, has shown a remarkable constancy, if not to say rigidity, in its academic structures.

It is only in a few universities that academic robes are still much in evidence, and the idea that the university stands *in loco parentis* to its students has been all but abandoned. Nevertheless, it is only with the rise of world-wide agitation against the traditional university system that we have had any reason to reflect on how little reason, other than tradition, there is for many academic institutions and practices. The fact that much in the prevailing university system of many countries does indeed represent an archaic order has made it hard for many university teachers and officials to recognize that the university revolt challenges not just academic traditions but the whole structure of society. University students, in contrast to other revolution-prone elements in society, do not belong to an economic or racial class which suffers oppression or discrimination. The contrary is true. In most Western countries (less so in France and Italy) the university student enjoys preferred treatment, great freedom and little responsibility. His material needs are met, often in relatively generous fashion, by public or private means. His personal freedom is limited only by the normal laws of society and by the threat of failure in his examinations, the latter of which in some cases is so infrequent as to cause only a last-minute burst of terror at the end of several lighthearted years, but no real self-discipline over a period of months or years. His nonstudent contemporaries in most cases either work or are in military service. Of course, many students do suffer real economic privation, but on the whole economic complaints are probably less serious than the psychological problem of increasing isolation in an impersonal structure. All in all, the lot of the student of today, both by comparison with nonstudents of the same age and with earlier university generations, does not seem a terribly hard one. Yet student rebellion is going on everywhere. Why is this the case? It has a superficial and a deeper cause.

The superficial cause which enables the university to become the field of action in which this new variety of race war, age war, can break out is simply the fact that the university student, particularly in the fields other than the technical, scientific, or legal, *is available*. He does not as yet have a position in society to lose. Thus he can take chances. His goals, from the nature of things, are long-range. If a mood comes to prevail that says that problems are supposed to be solved *now*, who will be easier to win for the task than someone who has time, who is occupied with intellectually tiring tasks and who has little really exhausting work to do as physical compensation, someone whose values are tied to a distant future and thus are unlikely to be destroyed by action he may take today? To the extent that the university student thinks about the world outside, the world *ahead of him in time*, he sees military service, economic problems, the necessity of working on a regular schedule, and so on—in short, he sees ahead of him what so many German student songs call "the life of Philistines." Better to agitate now, as a student, than to wait for the hard years ahead.

If we see that the student is *available*, that he is *suspicious of the future*, and that he has relatively *little to lose*, we can understand that he is a good subject for the appeal of the agitator. Even the spontaneous, relatively nonsensical student riots of fifteen years ago could always gather a crowd of enthusiasts at a moment's notice without any goal worthy of the name; how much more so today, when real issues have been brought into the open. Any group interested in changing society, whether more violently or less violently, would be foolish to ignore the vast explosive potential of a physically healthy, spiritually undernourished, morally outraged, and intellectually bored student generation with time on its hands. Naturally such groups do not ignore it.

A Deeper Reason: the Abdication of the Nobility. The university is a deeply tradition-conscious institution, and no tradition is more deeply rooted than that of the superior status and merit of its "nobles," the professors. The academic nobility, like the military nobility of an earlier age, had to fight to obtain its titles, and unlike the hereditary aristocracy of Europe, each new generation has had to fight again. But if the professors have not necessarily lost their true superiority vis-à-vis their students, i.e., their academic proficiency, they have lost the rationale for it and their confidence in it.

The university—in some respects this is true also of the church—has been living off of borrowed capital. What is in fact the rationale behind the intellectual enterprise? Surely it is the preeminence of the intellect over the world of nature. It is not necessary to fall into the Idealistic delusion that Mind is everything in order to recognize that Mind is something, and that it does have certain prerogatives over blind matter. The medieval Catholic university saw its task as one of understanding the Will and the Word of God, which gave order and meaning to the universe. The modern liberal university has seen its mission in terms of assuring progress by the progressive subjugation of nature under man, knowledge bringing power, and by guiding man through Reason. Both visions were, in short, *noetic*.

The last several university generations have been reverting to a biological vision. In this respect we will soon have to speak of the postliberal university. Progress in nature was believed to come through evolution; progress in society through class struggle. Both are directed by the power of the dialectic, far beyond the ability of man's conscious mind to master. The conscious mind itself in turn has been subjected to the devastating attacks of Sigmund Freud and of the behaviorists, often not fully or properly understood, so that our age can be termed one of a growing rejection of reason, indeed, of consciousness itself. Freud, in fact, sought to defend civilization by explaining the continuing struggle of the human consciousness against the dark forces beneath its surface, but his doctrines have led to the widespread conclusion that it was a lost cause from the outset.[5]

At the Uppsala Fourth Assembly of the World Council of Churches, sociologist Margaret Mead reproached a group of young radicals, saying, "You have absolutely no sense of history!" The argument was over the refusal of many youth participants to admit that anything that was accomplished by the so-called white liberals of Miss Mead's generation was worthwhile, and their failure to recognize the danger that their radical tacks would destroy what her generation had won. There was in her reproach something of the bitterness of Job's reply to his "miserable comforters," "No doubt you are *the* people, and wisdom will die with you"

[5] Cf. Philip Rieff, *Freud: The Mind of the Moralist* (New York: Viking, 1959), and Richard T. LaPiere, *The Freudian Ethic* (New York: Duell, Sloan, & Pearce, 1959). For the theme of the revolt against reason, see Arnold Lunn, *The Revolt against Reason* (London: Eyre & Spottiswoode, 1950), and Francis A. Schaeffer, *Escape from Reason* (London and Chicago: I.V.F., 1968).

(JOB 12:2). What frustration for an old campaigner, to be told by those who now enjoy the fruits of her victories that all her struggles were trivial!

To deny value to everything that has been accomplished in the past, to speak of today's society as *totally* unjust, is to deny the continuity of human existence and history. A totally unjust society would be quite difficult to design! Yet although the charge is foolish, it does have effects. Just as class struggle fragments mankind along economic lines and race struggle along racial lines, so age struggle fragments mankind along temporal lines. The age struggle may well never reach a peak of real violence like the other class struggles, because it cuts deeply into every kind of community, from the family to the nation, and ultimately cuts individuals off from their past and future. It does not need to break out into real violence, however; if it simply smoulders long enough, it will destroy the cohesion, based on mutual comprehension and confidence, that is necessary for the functioning of human civilization and society.

The age struggle would be an even more monstrous deceit if it should in fact turn out that it has originated not with the young who seek power and self-expression, but with the old who are manipulating them for their own ends, just as the old patriarch Mao Tse-tung has manipulated the young in his "Cultural Revolution." In a different way, the rapidly expanding youth market in clothing, books, music, etc., is less an expression of the spontaneous taste of the young than of the calculations of old marketing experts. It will likewise turn out to be a deceit if the young of today gain the power to smash existing structures and establish new ones, by which they maintain it in their own hands instead of passing it on. The movie *Wild in the Streets* imagines a situation in which retirement will be enforced at age thirty and concentration camps at age thirty-five.

But will those who at twenty-five had the vigor forcibly to retire and to incarcerate their own elders willingly accept the road to oblivion when they reach thirty? It seems highly unlikely.

Because it is so unlikely, it is perhaps unnecessary to take the age struggle seriously, as a principle, to its logical conclusion, and to imagine that progress requires every generation of adults to wander, willingly or by force, into oblivion at thirty. Such an eventuality might happen once, if one whole age group is so lacking in self-confidence and sense of responsibility as to permit it, but it will be as a means to quite a different end. That it should persist is as unlikely as the much-touted "permanent revolution." Nevertheless, it will still be instructive to look at what it implies. To emphasize only what is happening *Now* as having real value or offering opportunity in social affairs is to destroy the accomplishments of civilization. To emphasize only the prerogatives of age is to postpone life until it is declining; to emphasize only the impulses of youth is to reduce human existence to a merely biological rhythm. Although the age struggle stands under the aegis of the New Left, it is worth noting that the predominance of the biological over the rational was a characteristic feature of the Nazi ethos.[6] Here again we see the extremes meeting, with the New Left following the course charted by *Mein Kampf*. The *Jugendbewegung* in Germany was one of the currents that contributed to the rise of National Socialism.

If one sees only the present moment as the time of value and of action, while pouring contempt on the existing structures of society, one of two possibilities emerges. The first is the hope that the triumphant Now will become a kind of timeless millennium, a Thousand-Year Reich. In

[6] See Gérard Mendel, *La Révolte contre le père* (Paris: Payot, 1968), pp. 223–265.

other words, when all the worthless structures of the past have been shattered, then *the right structure* will emerge and will endure indefinitely. Such a "freezing" of society is the vision of George Orwell's 1984, in which the "perfection" of society will have made science superfluous and change impossible. This vision is dreadful for Orwell, and of course he is right. A millennium under any other ruler but God Himself would in effect be hell. The *right structure* would perpetuate itself, and history as such would cease. Does not this utopian vision have all the elements of tyrannical rigidity, to a much greater degree than they are present in tradition-encrusted bourgeois democracies? Is there really more dynamic change going on in Mao's China than in bourgeois Italy, for example? A Thousand-Year Reich does not seem very likely to be realized, for human society is always in ferment, yet it must not be denied that modern science makes possible new means of total control hitherto undreamed of. Even without technology, there have been static societies in the past. If by the smashing of today's structures we step into such a Reich, will we ever step out again? The destruction of our present democratic structures, with what Herbert Marcuse calls their "repressive tolerance," will inevitably lead to fastening a far more rigid and inflexible structure on all society. The question is, Will it be spontaneous, creative, free? Or will it be like Orwell's world of 1984? The evidence of human experience is in favor of Orwell.

The second alternative, that which is less likely to result from the present struggles but one which doubtless appeals more to a certain kind of mind, is the vision of perpetual revolution. The dream of perpetual progress expressed a faith in the triumph of man's reason independent of a divine plan. It emphasized the human *nous* instead of the Mind of God. The dream of perpetual revolution has no

nous at all. It is the dream of the triumph of purely biological energy over the mind.

In some ways the renunciation of all control by the mind
of man over social development is a logical consequence
of the loss of any sense of divine control or of a divine
plan in history. Without a sense of God's purpose, the
awareness of human moral responsibility is quickly replaced
by Darwinist and Marxist concepts of racial and social
evolution as the only "plan" for the species of man or by
Freudian or another kind of psychological determinism for
the individual. If this kind of blind determinism were in
fact true and did grasp the essential reality of human existence, then man's culture, his religions, his ethical systems, indeed all his dreams and aspirations would be only
smoke and mist. The material alone would be important,
as the biological world is more substantial than the noetic,
the world of the mind, with its analyses, its theories, its
syntheses and its ideals. If only the biological material has
validity, then under such circumstances, but only under
such circumstances, it is proper to claim absolute predominance for the young, for those in whom biological life is
at its peak. But then, why bother to claim it? Will it not
assert itself by biological drive, without any need for arguments drawn up by the mind?

The idea that the young should have nothing to say about
the conditions of their life, study, and other concerns is
one thing; the idea that they should have everything to
say is quite another. "Between them," as John Donne used
to say, "there is a fair way for a moderate man to walk in."
To give preeminence to biological vigor even in those areas
that are the realm of the mind in education, the sciences,
law, is to deny the mind and *to abandon the attempt of
the human intellect to come* to grips with the real world.
Christian thinkers from St. Paul onward have warned that

the mind of man cannot be trusted to attain unaided to the highest truths, but non-Christians have indignantly rejected such a dogmatic limitation on the autonomous powers of the human reason. How ironic that today the tools of reason should be used to denounce and destroy the control of reason over nature! Well has Herman Dooyeweerd called our age "the twilight of Western thought."

Radical students in Germany and elsewhere reject the "authoritarian" teaching system, perhaps not without reason. As an alternative, they are establishing (as also has happened in the United States) "free" or "critical" universities, in which the students teach each other. But what do they use as subject matter? Perforce they must use the deposit of mankind's intellectual *tradition*, most of it the product of "authoritarian" scholars over thirty, even if they read them only to criticize them! Where could they go, whom could they criticize, if all the heritage of authoritarian reactionary scholarship were to be destroyed? An attack on tradition as tradition (rather than as bad tradition) is an attack upon the activity of the mind, and upon the mind itself.

We have already noticed that even language is tradition. Thus it does not surprise us that the very structure of language should now be coming under attack. Languages have a natural rhythm of growth and change, but in many cases this rate is being artificially hastened. Old words are deliberately destroyed. For example, consider words like God, sin, virtue, honor, Christian; they have been almost entirely evacuated of content. New words and new expressions take their place, but not the same place, for all too often with the loss of the old word, the concept itself goes. The phenomenon of a new language for each new generation effectively inhibits all communication between the generations. It cripples the transmission of man's intellectual heritage. Of course one must be careful not to overreact against harmless slang; nevertheless, the problem is genuine. The importance of the attack on language for destroying tradition and establishing a new order was clearly recognized by Orwell in his discussion of "Newspeak" in 1984.

Orwell's Newspeak has parallels in both government jargon and the new language habits of the youth subculture. Of course a living language is always changing. But it can change too fast. Furthermore, the attack on language does not take place only within language. We are now all familiar with Marshall McLuhan's downgrading of the written word and of his praise for the nonverbal communication of the mixed media. He considers this "progress" and therefore desirable, freeing man from the bondage of linear thought. Yet at the same time he speaks of the return to "village" as opposed to town culture on a global scale, to a kind of retribalization. Is this not an abandonment of civilization, the very word for which we derive from *civis*, citizen (of a city)?

The final step is the exaltation of the drug experience. This is the end of all verbal communication. The history of the rise of Western science is the history of attempts of the human mind to understand, to utilize, and to control external reality. Many scholars have maintained that this attempt depended on the widespread acceptance of the Christian world-view, which teaches the reality and goodness of the created world, contrasting, for example, with Hindu thought, which sees the world perceived by the senses as a world of illusion. Whether or not this analysis is fully true, the gradual decline of Christian faith has been followed, with the passage of time, by a loss of a sense of the *importance* if not actually of the *reality* of the material world. There seems to be something hugely inconsistent in the fact that left-wing students who incline, following

Marx, to an extreme philosophical materialism, also agitate for the freedom to use drugs. Marx fought religion as "opium" for the people which kept them in bondage; some of his twentieth-century admirers paradoxically claim for the people genuine opium and its relatives as necessary to freedom!

What does all this mean? It is the attempt to retreat from all objective, logical structures to a world of dreams, the private world in which

> The mind is its own place, and in itself
> Can make a Heav'n of Hell, a Hell of Heav'n.
> John Milton, *Paradise Lost*, I:254–255

Those words were spoken in hell by the fallen archfiend. Later Milton's Satan, looking on the new-made world that God has created, is forced to recognize that he himself is the source of evil, and that he cannot make it different by dreaming: "Which way I flee is Hell; myself am Hell" (IV:75).

Milton's devil was forced to this conclusion by the sight of the beauty of the real world that he, being rational, could not deny. The drug experience, if carried to its logical conclusion, can make it impossible to see the real world and to reason coherently.

It is curious that it is also precisely the young, who have so much biological vigor with which to master the real world, and not the old, who are in the forefront of the drug clamor. This seems inconsistent with our thesis that the age struggle represents a return to the biological and a flight from the noetic. In fact, it is quite consistent with it. The young rebels intuitively must recognize that the material world can be mastered only by some variation of the intellectual enterprise as represented by science, technology, and the university. The unclouded reason cannot resist attempting this mastery, and it will not willingly forgo the tools developed and used by earlier generations. The only way to prevent the cold constraints of reason from coming back is to cloud the reason. The solution then is to take refuge in the irrational, in the drug sensation, the only thing which permits the mind to be "its own place, and in itself . . . [to] make a Heav'n of Hell, a Hell of Heav'n." Alas, the mind's heaven and the mind's hell, though often terribly real, are not the only ones: "It is appointed to men to die once, and after that comes judgment" (HEBREWS 9:27).

In the last analysis, then, the reaction against tradition destroys not only time but also space, the objective world. Man is freed from the "shackles" of traditional civilization, but nothing remains to him except the surge of biological life, which, burning itself out in man's third decade, will condemn him to decades of an empty future in which he is homeless and a stranger, and to an eternity of futile self-reproach.

6.

Struggle, Civilization, and Barbarism

THE class struggle today manifests itself in three principal ways: as the struggle between economic classes, between racial classes, and between age classes. We should not overlook the fact that in addition there is one more kind of class struggle, namely, that between the sexes: Women's Liberation. This is a very complex phenomenon,

---

* The gnostic mentality which prevailed in the Mediterranean basin during the first two centuries of the Christian era affected not only pagans, but also Jews and Christians. This very complex movement has been described by Hans Jonas in *The Gnostic Religion* (Boston: Beacon, 1965), and was vigorously attacked by St. Irenaeus of Lyons around 180 in his book *Against Heresies*. The Gnostics held that the world with all its structures was either the product of a degenerative process or the handiwork of a malicious sub-god called the Demiurge. As we have suggested earlier, Arnold Kuenzli, in a major study, "Karl Marx: A Psychograph" (*Karl Marx: Eine Psychographie* [Vienna, Frankfurt, Zurich: Europa, 1965]), identifies a similar hatred for created reality in Marx's mental make-up.

which we cannot consider in depth here, but because of its importance it is necessary to make certain observations.

The Women's Liberation movement exists and attracts support and criticism on two levels. On a more superficial level (but one of great importance to countless women), we must observe the fact that throughout history women have to a greater or lesser degree been treated as the wards of their male relatives. Without denying that there is far more to the "obedience" of a Christian wife to her husband than is suggested by the expression "submission," or that this relationship provides privileges and honor for the wife as well as for the husband, we can nevertheless admit that there is a good deal about which women may justly complain in the contemporary social structure. At this level, Christians will tend to support the cause of Women's Liberation.

There is, however, a deeper and far more problematic level to the Women's Lib movement. It may not be taken seriously by the majority of modern women, but it is there, like the dark fanaticism underlying Hitler's sometimes apparently praiseworthy policies such as full employment. At this level Women's Liberation is not directed against specific abuses, but against the very order of creation, together with its Creator. God Himself is rejected as "patriarchal," and Judaism and Christianity come in for special attack. The alleged reason is their use of the male pronoun for God (and for Jesus Christ as well, of course). In reality, however, the two biblical religions are being attacked for a much more fundamental reason, namely because they affirm and approve Creation as a work of God, and thus affirm the creation ordinances, among them the difference between man and woman, their differing roles in the family, etc. At this level we can call the movement "gnostic," by which we mean that it demonstrates a marked hostility to the created world and to its Creator. See Note* on page 116.

The deep hostility of many representatives of Women's Liberation to Christianity can only be understood with respect to this second, gnostic level, because on the practical level the Christian religion has accomplished more than any other force to elevate and dignify woman. A gnostic attitude has no interest in practical progress, however, but protests against the very existence of structures, in this case even against the creation ordinances of God. It is against this background that we must understand the support given by many Womens' Lib figures not only to homosexuality, but even to abortion, which seems to be a denial of the very essence of womanhood. In addition, of course, we note that certain currents in the movement are attached to the occult: the name WITCH (Women's International Terrorist Conspiracy from Hell) is more than a bit of black humor.

It is a curious—or should we say, diabolical?—coincidence that several disparate movements unite in their "racist" condemnation of the older male WASP: Black Power condemns the whites (a large majority); the New Left attacks those whites who are no longer young enough to be students, leaving a reduced majority; Women's Lib turns its fire upon those no-longer-so-young whites who are males, especially if they happen to subscribe to the Christian faith. Is it really possible that the middle-aged, male WASP population has behaved badly enough to deserve all this invective? It seems to me that there must be hidden motives of a much deeper nature, which we can only characterize as anti-Creation and in the last resort, diabolical. But we must leave this complex and serious question and return to the more general issue of the class struggle. In order for class tensions, which always exist, to break out into class struggle or class war, three conditions must be present: first, there must be persistent inequalities, or inequities which change too slowly between the classes; second, there must be a lack of real communication and community among the classes; third, the classes must be relatively fixed, so that members of one cannot easily pass into another.

We have seen that the traditional class struggle of Marxist theory, the economic struggle, is losing its power to bring about revolutionary social change in the industrialized world, simply because the inequities diminish rapidly. As a result, the less privileged classes think that they have more to gain by work than by revolt, while their most gifted members, their most effective leaders, rapidly rise into a more privileged class. The other two forms of class struggle have gained in importance as means to smash existing structures in the measure that economic class rivalries have declined in usefulness.

Racial inequities tend to hang on longer than economic ones, even in a rapidly improving economic structure, simply because race itself is a relatively permanent and unchangeable characteristic. Where racially based inequities have been legally abolished, as in the United States in recent years, prejudice still exists to be inflamed on both sides. The less favored race can be encouraged to demand punitive damages, a kind of discrimination in reverse, claiming them as its rightful due after centuries of bad treatment. The race which has hitherto enjoyed the favored position finds it hard enough to concede mere equality: reverse discrimination quickly leads to inflamed tempers and to charges that "they're trying to take us over." From this perspective, racial struggle offers fertile ground for the cultivation of persistent conflicts to crack an existing social structure.

Communication between different economic classes can be impeded by such superficial things as different accents. A person who has never known poverty may find it quite impossible to place himself in the position of someone who has—witness Marie Antoinette's famous suggestion, "Let them eat cake!" Nevertheless, economic class interests can be bridged by appealing to other factors, such as national feeling. Attempts to create international solidarity among the working classes and among the aristocrats against national interests failed in both world wars, however; workers fought against workers and aristocrats against aristocrats. National sentiments, a shared culture and tradition, proved far stronger than class divisions. The inhibiting effect of a common culture and common cultural heritage on class struggle is marked; the dynamics of class struggle, of whichever type, demand the destruction of national traditions and sentiment. Thus the repudiation of the cultural heritages in literature, art, and music, removes a vital inhibition.

The progressive destruction of national traditions is already quite advanced in the Western world. Only rarely, of course, is such destruction consciously planned with the intention of promoting internal class struggle. Often purely commercial interests are responsible. Whether it is by design or by chance, the effect is the same. A sense of community can last only where communication is good and where traditions are shared and honored; when a minority group within a nation feels itself cut off from or rejected by national traditions, it will be much readier to participate in a prolonged struggle with the majority than if it is conscious of a common if unequal heritage.

Communication is often rendered difficult by economic class distinctions, and racial differences pose an even greater hindrance. Enough has been said about differences between

Negro and European culture in the United States in recent
years to make it clear how difficult it is for the Negro to
understand the way a European-American thinks, and especially vice versa. The greater the emphasis which can be
placed on race as the primary factor with which an individual should identify, the more difficult it will be for other
traditional factors, such as political party, religion, or the
army, to command the joint loyalty of members of different
racial groups. Exacerbation of racial antipathy can lead only
to segregation and secession, and the latter can in all likeli-
hood be attained only through war, if at all.

When we come to the third form of class struggle, which
is in many ways the most paradoxical form, age struggle,
we face a puzzling situation in which the first principle
outlined above, that of persistent and lasting inequities,
does not seem to hold. If the young do not necessarily
receive increasing rights and privileges from their elders
while they are young, they gain them by the necessary
process of growing older. The inevitability that age will
bring the desired goal in a brief space of time sets a natural
limit to the periods of youthful militancy. For example, it
seems unlikely that an age group spanning more than about
three years will agitate for voting rights for eighteen-year-
olds.

Since the inequities between age groups are rapidly overcome by the inevitable process of growing older, how are
we to explain the violence of the age conflict as we experience it today? One reason is evident: since for any group
of young people the period during which it "suffers oppression" because of being young is naturally limited, anyone
who wishes to exploit such a sense of oppression must work
to sharpen and intensify it. To make anything out of the
age struggle, it must be brought to a head. For the young,
a gradual growth in awareness of their plight as members

of a less favored group cannot be allowed to grow over a long period of time, as is possible with racial sensitivities, because if a long period elapses, all the members graduate. A particular generation of youth must be made to think in class terms while there is time, i.e., before it passes beyond the pale into the sobriety of middle age. The need to move fast causes much of the frenzy which is evident in the politization of the youth subculture. If the young are not prevailed upon to respond in haste, they will not respond at all.*

There is an important factor which tends to prolong the inequities in the age gap, namely, the artificial prolongation of the period of adolescence (for want of a better word). As graduate study becomes more common and more prolonged, the "youth" group is enlarged at its upper edge. A similar extension has taken place in a downward direction. In America, "children" have practically ceased to exist, and even the words "boys" and "girls" are suspect terms (except as used by the middle-aged to refer to each other): only "young people" remain. Whether this development has been made inevitable because of earlier physical maturation brought on by better nutrition, or whether it has been promoted by such things as the commercial development and exploitation of the youth market, it certainly has taken place. It is remarkable that successful attempts have been made to create a feeling of community among those in the age group from fifteen to twenty-nine, despite

* Among people who have left the United States to avoid the draft, one often hears the remark, "I can't afford to waste two years of my life [in the army]." On the other hand, many of these same people have no compunctions about "dropping out" (of school, work, etc.) for an even longer period; one can see how the importance of time is felt only in certain connections and not in others. The young are not so averse to wasting time in general. It is to forestall youthful indolence that those who wish to profit by the age struggle must push their young disciples to an immediate peak of frenzy.

the very important physical, educational, and economic barriers which lie athwart that span of years. Does a young doctor of twenty-six have more in common with a senior resident of thirty-odd or with a high school junior of seventeen? To ask the question is to answer it. Yet the sense of a coherent "youth" culture embracing high schoolers and married Ph.D.'s does exist. (Of course, it exists least in the area of the example. The students who are studying *something*—medicine, engineering, natural science, even law and history—have been least involved in the phenomena of the age war, while those who are just "finding themselves" in English literature, philosophy, the arts, or even theology have been most involved.)

As the youth group has expanded and been given a perhaps unnatural sense of coherence, it has also progressively lost contact with or been cut off from its elders. This occurs not least through rapidly changing language. Just as a common language builds ties, lack of one destroys them. After the rise of Adolf Hitler, the German-speaking Swiss began to reemphasize their native Swiss German, a language virtually incomprehensible to the Germans, to underline their differences with Hitler's *deutsches Volk*. The attempt was on the whole successful, so successful that one wonders whether Switzerland will ever again make the contributions to German literature in the twentieth century that it did in the nineteenth. In like manner, the youth subculture of many countries is creating not only new words but almost whole new languages, making it quite hard for elders to communicate with the young. The childish desire to have a secret language of one's own, locking and unlocking the door to a private world into which only a select group can penetrate, which used to manifest itself in such things as pig-Latin, has now been fulfilled to a singular degree. People who do not make it their business to keep in close contact with teenagers may find their language less understandable than pig-Latin when they do try to communicate with them.

Another aspect of the language issue is reflected in the adoption by the youth and by the race struggle groups of the language of class struggle. German students, for example, enjoying government scholarships and "academic freedom" unrivaled anywhere in the world, borrow the language of Marx and of Mao to express their antagonism to the society that pampers them. Likewise Negro militants use Marxist language to arouse the Negro bourgeoisie against the white bourgeoisie and the Negro proletariat against the white proletariat. All of this goes to show that in each of these aspects of the class struggle, the possibility of a solution attracts the militants far less than the goal of *perpetuating divisions* and of *preventing communication*. The real goal is to smash what now exists.

In other words, the motif of class struggle comes to dominate over the goals which the class struggle seeks to achieve. This phenomenon is not unique, of course. In World War II, many German officers knew long before the end that they were not fighting to win; they were fighting merely to be able to go on fighting longer. When Marshall McLuhan coined his slogan, "The medium is the message," he found an apt phrase to characterize a situation in which means become their own ends. In the absolutization of the class struggle that we are witnessing today, the struggle as means becomes the struggle as end: "permanent revolution" is the 1984-like slogan of some of the most rigid societies the world has ever known, societies in which no one is as free as the average household slave was in imperial Rome. To say "the medium is the message" is to say that intellectual content is not important, and this is precisely what happens as the biological reasserts itself over the noetic. Contrary to Teilhard de Chardin's vision of a spiritualization of the biological world, we are confronted with an animalization of the spiritual world.

CLASS STRUGGLE AND CIVILIZATION

The great civilization of the classical world fell from a variety of causes, not the least of which was the repeated pressure of barbarian invasions. Looking at the Roman Empire during the reign of Marcus Aurelius (161–180), or even later, after it had been severely shaken by civil disorders but revived by the energy and determination of Diocletian (284–305), one would have thought that it possessed the resources, the administrative ability, and the superior civilization necessary to withstand the barbarians indefinitely. Yet finally it collapsed rather abruptly. Civilization did not possess the will or moral courage to resist the onrush of barbarism. Writing over one hundred years ago, the historian Lord Macaulay predicted that democratic America would fall to barbarians as imperial Rome had done, but with this difference: Rome's barbarians were invaders from beyond the imperial frontiers; America would create and raise her barbarians within her own borders. In the United States today, the outlines of a rebirth of barbarism are clear for all to see—and not only in the United States, but in many other countries as well. The will to resist is as paralyzed in democratic Europe and America as it was in imperial Rome; this paralysis comes in large measure from a widespread acceptance of the class struggle and of the philosophy behind it. No one wants to oppose destiny.

The class struggle, in its triple form, is a struggle against civilization, against the long struggle of man to be something other than barbaric. The class struggle is the abolition not only of community but also of communication, the end of civilization and the reestablishment of barbarism. The very word barbarian (Greek *barbaros*) is traditionally derived from the supposed inability of the barbarian to communicate in rational language: his speech was the repetition of meaningless sounds: bar—bar—bar . . . Of course the "barbarians" with whom the ancient Greeks had to deal also had perfectly good languages, but meaningful communication between them and the Greeks was nonexistent.

A lack of communication is not the *only* cause for internecine struggle, for civil wars are often the worst wars, and surely the differences between West Germany and East Germany do not depend on lack of linguistic understanding. However, where there is no common language, there is no possibility that one group can appreciate the cultural values of the other.

In an interview with the "Living Theatre" on French television, its director, Julian Beck, stated that it was the purpose of his group "to destroy the steel structure of laws which civilization has erected to protect itself from barbarism."[1] The hope, expressed or unexpressed, in such an attitude is that if the present order, being unjust, is smashed, somehow a new order will drop into its place. It ought to be quite unnecessary even to discuss this strange hope, so contrary to everything experience teaches us. When in this world's history has the violent smashing of an old order of society *ever* led to a more equitable new order?

The American Revolution was one "revolution" which precisely did not smash the existing society. This is the reason why the example of the American Revolution has no particular meaning to the radically inclined revolutionaries of today. The French Revolution offers a much better example of a smashing of structures, although even the French Revolution, after its initial phase, left the economic system largely intact. The society which resulted from the

[1] *La Tribune de Lausanne*, October 13, 1967.

American Revolution was not less just than that which preceded it, but neither was it much more just; the War of Independence is a better name for the conflict out of which the United States was born than the American Revolution. The democracy that ultimately arose out of the bloody chaos of the French Revolution may be considered better than the *ancien régime,* and if this is granted, we can look on the French Revolution as an example of a better order "dropping" into the place of a worse one that had been smashed. Of course, the new order in France did not come directly from the Revolution, but was preceded by the Terror, by Napoleon's wars, and finally was imposed on that country by the powers which defeated Napoleon. The examples of more recent revolutions, from the Russian through the Cuban, do not give us much reason to hope that the order which rises out of revolutionary chaos will bring more justice than the one which preceded it.

Whence then this hope that destruction of existing structures will lead to better ones? That the hope exists cannot be denied: nowhere has it been expressed more purely than in the 1968 French riots, when the black flag of anarchy was raised at the Sorbonne as the alternative to the tricolor of Gaullist France. Here again was a strange triumph of unreason. What in fact could have resulted from the collapse of General de Gaulle's Fifth Republic? The *société de consommation* would have gone. The students had no clear idea of what would have taken its place, but something would have been improvised, as Lenin improvised his revolution in Russia. Would that something have provided greater freedom than de Gaulle's France? Likewise the American and the German SDS (Students for a Democratic Society in the U.S.A.; Sozialistischer Deutscher Studentenbund in Germany) seem to have only vague ideas of what will replace the university or the society which they hope to destroy, but there would be nothing vague about their system if it triumphed.

This hope, that out of chaos a better society might come, on any sober evaluation, appears not merely vain but absurd. That it should fire the imagination of so many, especially among the young, in so many societies, demonstrates better than anything else the spiritual bankruptcy of present-day Western democratic societies and their abject failure to gain the confidence and loyalty of their students and other young people. This failure is most dramatic at a time when material prosperity and the opportunity of receiving a higher education are more widespread than at any time in the past. In other words, the hope is so irrational and so ill-founded that it constitutes a terrible indictment of present-day society. So many of society's most favored people feel that it must be destroyed *at any cost*. Of course, one reason why they feel thus is that their elders, obsessed with a guilty awareness of their own lack of principles, make no effort to defend the existing order. That there are much hypocrisy and evil embodied in the present Western social and economic order is too patent to be denied, but a guilty paralysis is not the cure for it. The question is not whether to hold tenaciously to all that we have, or to smash it all and hope for better, but to bring the tools of the intellect and the standards of the Christian faith to bear on the present situation so that good may come out of it.

THE END OF COMMUNICATION: THE CRISIS OF THE WORD

A true class struggle can break out only when all communication has broken down between the classes. Precisely such a general breakdown of communication is becoming an increasingly profound symptom of the world in which we live. Words have lost their meanings in so many situations that it has become virtually impossible to make an unambiguous statement. One example will be given from the political realm, one from the theological.

One of the most remarkable naval operations of 1968, unique in American history, was the seizure by North Korean naval units of the U.S.S. *Pueblo* in international waters on January 23. Even more remarkable were the means adopted by the United States to secure the release of the *Pueblo*'s captain and crew. Eleven months later, on December 22, Major General Gilbert H. Woodward, the chief United States negotiator at Panmunjom, signed a statement to the effect that the United States acknowledged "grave acts of espionage committed by the U.S. ship against the Democratic People's Republic of Korea." Immediately beforehand, General Woodward declared, "The document which I am going to sign was prepared by the North Koreans, and is at variance with the above position [i.e., with the United States' claim that the *Pueblo* was not engaged in illegal activity], but my signature will not and cannot alter the facts."[2]

In order to free its seamen, the United States government made a formal statement which it branded in advance as false. Few will dispute the U.S. government's responsibility to secure the freedom of the *Pueblo*'s men, but, as the French newspaper *Le Monde* commented, it marked an unprecedented new low in governmental hypocrisy; perhaps it can be compared with the performance of Russia's ambassador to the United Nations, who, in the unusually frank language of *Le Figaro*, "coldly lied" to the General Assembly about the invasion of Czechoslovakia. Admitting

[2] Cited in *U.S. News and World Report*, January 6, 1969, p. 31.

the great moral pressure placed on the United States to free the men being thus held as hostages, the *Pueblo* affair raises the question: if not only Soviet diplomats but even American ones solemnly and publicly lie, knowing that everyone else knows they are lying what remains of truth in government pronouncements?

A religious example could be given from the writings of any one of a number of different contemporary theological luminaries. Let us consider only the efforts made by certain "modern" or "secular" theologians to show how when the Apostles spoke of the resurrection of Jesus, they did not intend to make a statement about anything that had actually happened, but were speaking of their own response to a "discernment situation." Paul van Buren and Willi Marxsen are examples of this type of "interpretation." Eric Mascall justly comments, "This seems to be quite extraordinarily perverse."[3] It is not only perverse, but anti-logical: antilogical not merely because it goes against the rules of logic, but because it goes against the rules of speech (Greek *logos*, word).

According to a fundamental statement of Christianity, "In the beginning was the Word" (JOHN 1:1). It was the divine Word which acted creatively to bring light out of darkness and order out of chaos. God *said* "Let there be light," and light was (GENESIS 1:3). By refusing to allow religious leaders such as St. Peter and St. Paul to use ordinary language tell us something about *facts*, instead of merely about their own "discernment situations," theologians of this type destroy the word itself: language is no longer allowed to bring light or order. The universe, created and ordered by the Word of God, will not fall into disorder because man destroys his own words, but if man deprives

[3] Eric L. Mascall, *op. cit.*, *p.* 83. See Paul van Buren, *The Secular Meaning of the Gospel* (New York and London: S.C.M., 1963), esp. Ch. 5.

all his words of their meanings, he will plunge himself and his social, economic, and intellectual structures into chaos. The meaningful *logos* of coherent speech will be replaced by the meaningless bar—bar—bar of the barbarians.

Only a few years ago, Protestants effectively polemicized against the Roman Catholic Church because its liturgy was celebrated in Latin, which not many worshippers could understand. At that time the Roman church, using bilingual missals, was in fact making an effort to see to it that worshippers did understand the Mass. Today, however, we have a plethora of new pseudoreligions that pride themselves on their exotic, unintelligible prayers and expressions.

The struggle against the heavy hand of traditionalism has taken on the grotesque and monstrous form of an attack on the very *process of tradition,* that is, on the handing down of values and of knowledge of every kind. It reaches its peak of frenzy in attacks on language itself. We may be amused at the efforts of the French Academy to protect the French language from the inroads of *Franglais,* but if the Academy is overly sensitive, its zeal is in a good cause. Without a reasonably stable language, nothing can be handed down, and culture—since it cannot be created anew by each school generation—must disappear.

The prospect that a whole modern language may disappear is unlikely, of course. Yet we have already seen that within an existing language, certain kinds of expression can be rendered useless for communication. In English, religious language has been made so ambiguous by "liberal" and "secular" appropriation of old terms in changed meanings that it is very hard to use it meaningfully. The language of patriotism, of honor, and of absolutes has in general suffered a similar fate. It is curious that the slogans and concepts of Marxism have preserved a certain vitality in the general debasement of language, although even in

Marxism, words come to convey less and less real content. What is a people's democracy? On the recent twentieth anniversary of the establishment of communism in Albania, Albanian government spokesmen prided themselves on the "fact" that their society has been "revolutionary" for twenty years.

Tradition can be one of the greatest barriers to a tyrannical exercise of power. The great King of Persia was forced to comply with his own decrees, "according to the law of the Medes and the Persians, which cannot be revoked" (DANIEL 6:8), even when he did not wish to do so. Tradition can also be a dead hand, impeding progress, inhibiting social justice, preventing talented individuals from achieving that of which they are capable. The problem is evidently one of *discrimination*, but this very word is suspect. To discriminate, one must be able to identify, to make distinctions, to compare, to select, and all this requires language concepts, thought-patterns, and traditional value structures. To say that traditions should be eternal and immutable is to shackle all progress. Such traditions have never existed, yet often those which do exist have been all too rigid. But to say that traditions may not exist is to say that civilization may not exist.

There are traditions which are so well respected and so generally accepted that it is unnecessary to defend them. As these lines are being written, the rector's office of the University of Geneva has just been freed from an "occupation" by two hundred students (February 27–March 3, 1969). There was no broad student support for the occupation, and apparently the authorities preferred to let the "occupiers" get tired of their game before asking them to leave. A group of farm boys and girls who were exhibiting domestic animals near the occupied university offices, posted a sign reading, "Additional donkeys and oxen, protesters, on display inside," with an arrow pointing to the university building.

In Switzerland the traditions of public discussion and dialogue are so deeply rooted that they cannot be swept away by a moment's "direct action." Even so, there seems to be the distinct possibility that a small but determined minority of students in Zurich, despairing of getting their hoped-for reforms by democratic process, may decide to close the university there. Switzerland has a tradition of democratic discussion, but can discussion defend that tradition against those determined to secure their demands not by persuasion, but by force? If such a question must be asked even in Switzerland, which has the stablest and strongest tradition of direct democracy in all the world, what must be said about other countries? The common sense and political sagacity of the Swiss are such that even liberally inclined or leftward-learning papers like the Zurich *Weltwoche* at once saw the real alternative posed by the attack on the university. The *Weltwoche*, although it largely sympathizes with the desire for a thorough-going university reform, entreated the students not to take forcible action against the university administration.[4] Its counsel is sage, but even in democratic Switzerland there are students who do not want to reform but to destroy the "bourgeois university" and with it bourgeois society. In Switzerland, economic class rivalry and racial sentiments are weak; perhaps only "age war" can threaten Swiss society. Whether such age war results from outside agitation or from inner decay, it is equally serious. In the attack on the Swiss bourgeois university and its *democratic* traditions, we can clearly see the tendency of age war to pass rapidly from an attack on certain traditional social structures as outmoded to an attack on the transmission of values itself,

4 *Die Weltwoche*, February 20, 1969.

with all that such an attack implies for the fragile edifice of human civilization.

Hypocrisy and its Cost. The widespread repudiation of existing structures in the area of education, a repudiation so total that it would gladly overthrow all that we now have without giving reason to hope that something better could come of it, is a clear indictment of the hypocrisy and injustice that have been built into the structures and into the whole system out of which they spring. This is the high cost now being paid by Western society for having become so hypocritical that it has lost the confidence and even the tolerance of a significant segment of its youth and has only meager support from the rest.

The fact of widespread hypocrisy in our institutional life cannot be denied, nor can the reality of the terrible penalty now being paid, that is, the distrust and alienation of a whole generation. Nevertheless, the failure of the present bourgeois democracies to resemble the Kingdom of God must not blind us to the fact that the alternatives to them may be still closer to the Kingdom of Evil. If slavery is an evil, well: by the standards of classical slaveholding societies, all the citizens of the so-called people's democracies are slaves. And it may well be that the utopia that would have resulted from the success of the May riots in France, or would be created by the SDS in America, might have been still harsher than the allegedly "mellowing" Communist regimes.

The rebellious proponents of age war have two things on their side: (1) the guilty conscience of the older generation that *knows* it has not done all things well; (2) the fact that the older generation itself has for the most part no higher ideal than its own comfort. By coming out for principles now, it might have to sacrifice comfort. Two generations ago there was a tremendous theological difference between the orthodox and the liberals of Christendom. It was the difference between supernaturalism and naturalism, between Christ the divine-human Savior and Jesus the Good Teacher. Despite the magnitude of this difference, almost everyone shared the same ideas on morality. A Yankee New Englander might be an orthodox Congregationalist, a Unitarian, or a high church Episcopalian; it would make little difference to his moral sense. As a result of this moral consensus across theological diversity, morality was taken more or less for granted, as a "given" of the total cultural situation. This consensus morality has been eroded on both the practical and theoretical fronts. Widespread wars, quick prosperity, deflation, inflation, depression, and millions of *nouveaux riches* have reduced the holders of the old consensus to a silent minority. The collapse of orthodox theologies, both Protestant and Catholic, has destroyed morality's theoretical foundation except among the minorities who still believe in orthodox Christianity. It should not surprise us, then, that the traditional words of the older generation carry little weight. But without valid words, there is neither civilization nor religion.

7.

Reformation

REVOLUTION OR
REPRESSION?

THE option that seems to offer itself to the Western democracies—the United States, France, and West Germany prominent among them—is the choice between revolution and repression. Repression is very much a live option, for these immensely wealthy societies, despite their failures and their persistent problems, have built up an immense reservoir of tangible assets that most of their citizens want to conserve, and large numbers would advocate and help enforce a brutal repression of all dissent rather than see their hard-earned assets stolen, sacked, or destroyed. A police-state or military-dictatorship type of repression might permit the upper and middle classes to preserve their material assets, but would be destructive of those spiritual values that depend on freedom. Despite what the New Left says about the crass materialism of the bourgeoisie, many members of the middle classes would not want to preserve their material assets at the cost of a total loss of spiritual values of freedom and all that goes with it. This residual quality of libertarian idealism is something on which the advocates of radical protest have successfully gambled, whether consciously or not. The method is to make the protest against the existing order so radical that people are faced with a choice between tyrannical repression on the one hand and anarchic revolution on the other. If forced to choose between such alternatives, large elements of the middle and upper classes, including many intellectuals, will opt for revolution—or at least permit it—rather than encourage a repression which runs counter to their every cherished memory of liberty. Of course, the paradox is that the "anarchic" revolution will promote neither liberty nor anarchy; the admirers of Che Guevara and Mao Tse-tung proclaim sexual anarchy and freedom to take drugs, but neither is available in Red Cuba or China.

The Radicalization of the Available Choices. On the side of the New Left there certainly are many people who are tremendously ignorant, irresponsible, or stupid, who really do believe that if the iron mold of civilization is shattered, something beautiful will automatically drop out. These see no harm in radicalizing the situation of class conflict, in giving society only the choice between radical revolution and authoritarian repression. The fact that this is a dishonest choice, that the revolution would be followed not by anarchy but by tyranny, does not matter to the ignorant, naive, and stupid, and their support is a valuable aid to those who know exactly what they want, to the future tyrant lords of the revolution. A radicalization of the choice is also sought by some conservatives, in the hope that the large, usually inert mass of the general public will be alarmed by the prospect of revolutionary chaos and choose a conservatively administered repression. Here too there is danger, for tyranny is tyranny, by whomever it may be administered. The conservatism which rides into power on the fear of left-wing violence may bring a violence of its own.

As long as the choice open to a society is between authoritarian repression and revolution and nothing else, there is no way to preserve the spiritual values either of Christianity or of humanistic liberalism. Those who realize this will see the necessity of breaking out of the dilemma, of providing another choice. Despite the difference in theory and in rhetoric, for a free society the choice between authoritarian repression and revolution is like asking with which of a bull's two horns one would prefer to be gored: both are fatal. Thus France's General de Gaulle, confronted with the events of May 1968 which brought France to the verge of civil war, sought to introduce a new possibility: the slogan of *participation* (and also, later, of regionalism) was intended to offer a way out of the impasse by means other than the ones which lead to tyranny by terror from the Left or to tyranny by repression from the Right.

Avoiding the issues. Whether de Gaulle's attempt, late in his career, to provide a third option will be carried on by his successor to extricate France from the difficulties with which his government failed to cope, only time will show. Whether his solution will prove adequate or not, one thing is clear: his diagnosis was right. The choice between revolution and repression is an issue that must be avoided: it is an either-or test in which both options are wrong. The only hope for freedom lies in finding a different option, another choice, one which will be constructive and creative, rather than one between compulsion and chaos. In order to offer a constructive, creative option it is necessary to break out of the rigid frame introduced by purely materialistic values. As long as people think that they can satisfy the emptiness in their lives by bread alone, their attempts to do so will become progressively more desperate and their actions progressively more extreme. The choice is not what C. P. Snow called it, one between "jam today" (revolution, in this case) and "jam tomorrow," but between food for the body only and food for both body and soul. The box with two exits, repression and revolution, does not represent the real choice which faces man. It is rather the absence of real choice, the tyranny which, without God, men cannot help but impose upon themselves and all their fellows. The revolution-repression choice is not a real choice at all, for the person who sees only this alternative has already chosen materialism; materialism, in turn, has no place for man's soul and knows nothing of freedom. In the materialistic framework the only choices to be made concern (1) who will administer the tyranny, and (2) whether the tyrant will rule with an iron fist or a velvet glove.

In short, the issue: revolution or repression? must be avoided at all costs, for it is a dilemma, both of whose horns will kill.

REVOLUTION OR REFORMATION

The true alternative must be one which means a real choice, not the mock choice between Fascist-style and Communist tyranny. In order to make such an alternative available, those who realize its importance must do all that is in their power to prevent the radical narrowing of the available choices down to those two that both spell tyranny and terror. The constant objection must be made: that is no real choice! The repression-revolution choice is truly *diabolical*. Both of its "options" are dictated by diabolos, the divider. One choice is to take the part of the haves against the have-nots, the other the reverse, but both follow the diabolical principle of dividing mankind and promising men that by dealing with a certain class of humans, qualified as beasts, they will escape the need to deal with the beast within themselves. Thus men will be cut off from each other, and their mutual hatred and condemnation will isolate them all from God.

As long as he looks only at the temporal horizon, i.e., at this present world, man cannot avoid the awareness of being bound, a prisoner. Not even the endless expanse of outer space can free him from the limitations placed on man by the brevity of man's life and his preoccupation with himself. The whole universe with all its countless prizes is not enough to fill the longing emptiness in a creature who was made to be the child of his Creator. The words of Deuteronomy, repeated by Jesus in His desert conflict with the Adversary of our race, are as true today as they were then, "Man shall not live by bread alone, but by every word that proceeds from the mouth of God" (MATTHEW 4:4, citing DEUTERONOMY 8:3). The Word of God comes to man from beyond time and space; it alone gives him a true alternative, the possibility of *reformation*. The Word of God presents us with a unique perspective. It speaks of a fallen but basically good world, a world which will be blasted and turned to evil as long as it is manipulated by the clever but corrupt mind of fallen, unregenerate man. It also presents the path of *reformation*, by which man and the world can be restored to beauty, strength, and love. There must be regeneration of the individual, through which his twisted spirit can be reformed in the true image of his Creator. Through the regeneration and re-formation of individuals, society and its structures can be reformed.

The word *reformation* in this context has nothing to do with Roman Catholic–Protestant Reformation polemics. It refers to a vision shared by both Protestants and Catholics who take their faith seriously: that God can take weak and evil men and make them good and strong, and through them, society. It does not refer simply to moral improvement, but to a remaking of man in conformity with God's purpose and plan. When any church, Protestant or Catholic, despairs of the re-forming power of God's Word and His grace working within individuals, then it naturally turns to trying to compel them by outside force. Then the church too faces the fatal choice between revolution and repression. Many church leaders are choosing for revolution, because they sense in the alternative of repression the materialistic concerns which Jesus condemned. What they fail to see is that in accepting the revolution-repression dilemma as the choice, they have already been gored by the bull of materialism.

This is not to say that there is no difference, or no significant difference, between the self-seeking conservationalist materialism of the possessors and the self-seeking revolutionary materialism of the dispossessed. There are differences, but it is not these differences which are decisive. Authoritarian repression accepts the given as good, and denies that evil exists, or that radical change is ever necessary. It would perpetuate the evil results of man's Fall, and fasten them by iron shackles upon our race forever. The power of a potential repression should not be underestimated: for the first time in human history, the technological tools are available to forge chains which will bind everyone and everything, and which will not necessarily rust or fall off with age. The early dictators of republican Rome accepted dictatorial powers for a limited period only. Later dictators refused to surrender them, thus becoming emperors, but the machine of imperial repression gradually grew old and creaky and finally ceased to function. Today our technology is better: the Roman Empire lasted less than four full centuries, with interruptions, but modern chains, once fastened, might bind mankind forever, or for as long as human history shall run.

Authoritarian repression, exercised with modern techniques and not tempered by any memory of the God to whom the princes of this world will one day answer, will perpetuate all the injustices man has perpetrated since his Fall. Revolution, by contrast, accepts the evil condition of creation, but denies that man himself is fallen or at fault. It places the whole blame on a class, members of which are not really recognized as men. "Free man," revolution says, "from all that restrains him and from his oppressors, and he will create peace, and justice, and harmony." Faced with such a statement, the conservative usually asks the question of performance: Are fifty-odd years of such "revolutionary" rule not yet enough to show us that those words have lost all meaning, and that revolution frees man from a cruel corruption only to make him fall more tragically?

There is a more basic objection, however. Revolutionary governments might very well perform better and permit more liberty than those of the "people's democracies" do at present, but as long as they operate on the principle that good can come by purging mankind of evil classes, and that they know which classes are evil, they claim omniscience and perpetuate the Fall. Bourgeois societies, especially as they retain some awareness of God, know that they are far from perfect; revolutionary societies do not. Denying that man has fallen, they blind themselves and bind themselves even more tightly to a destiny which deprives man of every vestige of freedom and dignity. Although the United States has never been a true revolutionary society, twentieth-century America thought of itself as a secular Promised Land ("thine alabaster cities gleam, undimmed by human tears . . ."). If there had been greater humility and more self-analysis and criticism in American education and public life in the first half of this century, there would be less tendency to self-abasement and self-condemnation today.

For a bourgeois society threatened by revolution, repression is not the answer, because it hardens the existing evils, if possible forever. Revolution would replace the old evils, unequally distributed, with which so many have learned to live, with a reign of equal evils for all: remember that according to the standards of ancient slaveholding societies, *every* citizen of a "people's democracy" is a slave. The answer lies only in *reformation*, in a word, in accepting the goodness but fallenness of creation and of man, so aptly described in God's Word, and in bringing to bear upon them the reforming power of that Word. Revolution is to a corrupt society what suicide is to a bad man: it shuts doors forever. What both need is reformation, not in the sense of moral reform, but reformation in the truest sense of the word. *Reformatio* does not mean a reshaping of the external appearance, but a recovery of the inner *forma*, the creative principle which formed the inert mass and gave it its character. At the origin of the world, God's word of command gave form to chaos: "The earth was without form and void . . . and God said, 'Let there be light' " (GENESIS 1:2–3). It is the same Word which Jesus flung in the teeth of the diabolos when he tempted Him to put bread for Himself ahead of God's purposes (MATTHEW 4:1–11); the Word is Jesus Himself, the Incarnate Word, who made the world (JOHN 1:3), who upholds the universe by the word of His power (HEBREWS 1:3), and who makes us free indeed, through a knowledge of the truth, if we continue faithfully to listen to Him (JOHN 8:31f).*

---

* "If you continue in my word, you are truly my disciples, and you will know the truth, and the truth will make you free." The second half of this sentence is probably the one saying of Jesus most often quoted out of context (as for example on one of the gates to the Harvard Yard in Cambridge, Massachusetts) to claim His support for the delusion that mere knowledge brings freedom. From the context, and from Jesus' other teachings (e.g., "I am . . . the Truth," JOHN 14:6), it is clear that the truth that makes free is the truth that He represents, i.e., the truth of the Word of God.

Only by a revelation coming from beyond our horizon, i.e., only by the Word of God, can we obtain a knowledge of the ultimate purposefulness of human existence. Only the Word of God and the faith that is a knowledge of and confidence in the truths the Word reveals can give us the inner *form* necessary for order, justice, and peace. Only those who hear this Word as God speaks to them in His prophets and apostles and in His Son have what is necessary to reform society and to make, as Christians daily pray, His will to be done on earth. Only with a reliable Word from God can we know His will and purpose. St. Paul wrote to St. Timothy that the Scripture, inspired by God, was able "to instruct you for salvation . . . ," but also that it would teach, reprove, correct, and train him in righteousness, so that he might be complete, equipped for every good work (II TIMOTHY 3:15–17). Only the Word of God makes one "wise unto salvation," but not only that: only the Word of God can give an inner structure to human society to make unnecessary the tyrannical impositions of repression or revolution. If this temporal world is all that there is, then anything can be justified in the name of making the best out of it that can be made; it is only in the light of eternity that the value of things in time takes on its true perspective.

REVELATION AS THE CHRISTIAN'S POSSESSION AND CALLING

For the Christian the Word of God is more than a means of access to personal salvation; it is an insight into the mystery of the will of God, into His plan for the fulness of time, applicable to all things in heaven and on earth (EPHESIANS 1:9f). The primary necessity of Christians today is to realize what a priceless possession is theirs as a people called out* by the voice of God. First comes the recognition that they have a unique privilege; then comes the consequence, the second duty, i.e., to fulfill its challenge, to accept their calling. Only as conscious *hearers* and *obeyers* of the Word of God is this to be done; only in the confidence that comes from knowing that they have a divine calling will Christians gain the necessary strength to fulfill that calling. All of the shouting done at the churches and within the churches about going into the world, meeting the world, is worse than idiocy until the churches and individual Christians know who and what they are. Consequently, knowledge of the Word of God is required, in order to know the calling of God; reflection upon and study of this calling are necessary to make it really a part of the Christian's self-understanding. Logically, hearing and understanding the calling are prior to accepting and obeying it, but from the perspective of time, accepting the calling must be done almost in the same breath as receiving it. We breathe in the inspired Word, and breathe out the obedient response. To hold it too long, like holding one's breath, is fatal.

The Word of God makes it possible for the Christian to say a definite No! to all revolution and to say it with a clear conscience, knowing that he is not opposing revolution by claiming that he has never been guilty of causing or tolerating social injustice, but because it contradicts God's revealed will. An awareness of his own past, of his own share in human injustice, should not paralyze the Christian as it does the secular bourgeois or liberal intellectual, making him submit supinely to the onrush of revolution because he knows that he is not blameless where oppression and exploitation are

---

* The church is the *ekklesía*, the called-out assembly (from *ek*, out of, and *kaléo*, call), summoned by the Word which it has heard to be a distinctive people, a "royal priesthood" to proclaim God's wondrous deeds (I PETER 2:9). Naturally the church in this sense refers, in St. Peter's words, "to you therefore who believe" (I PETER 2:7).

concerned. The Word of God says that it is *His* kingdom which is to come, and that it is to come not by violent revolution but by *reformation* and *regeneration*. In today's violent social change, where all the foundations are shaking, the Christian must live up to his heritage and proclaim that true freedom and a life worthy of humanity come not by violence, not by the revolutionary smashing of structures, but by reformation according to the Word of God, beginning with individuals. There are no shortcuts; there are many wrong roads.

The No to Revolution and the Duty to Reformation. There are few privileges without duties. Jesus said, "To whom much is given, of him will much be required" (LUKE 12:48). Alone among the peoples, classes, and groups in this world, the Christian knows the purpose and goal of human existence. Because he knows what God's purpose is, he alone can say a justified No to revolution; he *must* say it, for to witness to God's purposes means to protest against the plan of Satan to cause men to wage eternal civil war. In the present situation where revolution is presented as the road to Utopia, the Christian must brand this hope as a fatal delusion and must refuse to share, support, or indulge it. He need have no qualm that in so doing he is seeking merely to protect his own assets, for this No is commanded by God. God's kingdom shall rule through the reforming and regenerating Word, not through the revolutionary tribunal, guillotine, or firing squad. God's purpose is to have children who will obey him out of understanding and love; even if a revolution could enforce the moral law of the Bible upon all, this would not fulfill His will. (Of course, the problem is not so simple, because if a government really tried to enforce biblical principles of law and justice before many of its citizens were *persuaded* that they should follow them, it would have a revolution on its hands. Biblical morality is difficult even for the believer in Christ, and it is dreadfully onerous to the unbeliever.) Since so many schemes to enforce Utopia are afoot today, the Christian must confront them all with a loud and distinct No!

The Affirmation after the Negation. God usually says No in order to say Yes to something better. "Thou shalt have no other gods before Me" is a No to make a Yes possible. Idols are forbidden in order to make it possible to worship the God of Mercy, Justice and Love. Without the No to false gods, men would not rise above idolatry. The No to revolution is similarly the prerequisite for a Yes, a command, an obligation. Precisely because the Christian must shout the No, he must hasten to say the Yes. It is almost worse than not speaking at all to say only No, for it deprives men of dangerous, vain hopes, which is good, but it gives them no true hope and this breeds despair. Earlier in this chapter, violent revolution and authoritarian repression were repeatedly paired for joint condemnation.

Why do we now stress the divine No only against revolution, saying nothing of repression? Does this mean that revolution is condemned so that the propertied Christian may conserve, by repression, those benefits which he would otherwise lose? Have we come back to religion as "opium for the people," so that the wealthy may live in tranquillity?

No, the difference does not lie in any superiority of repression to revolution. Both are wrong, but wrong in different ways. One is an evil vigor, the other an evil languor. Revolution, like the Moloch of the Carthaginians, is a cruel idol which consumes the children of those who serve it, generation after generation. How many East German teenagers have been sacrificed to the Moloch of revolution at the Berlin Wall? How many young Czech and Slovak lives have been consumed to preserve the "accomplishments" of the Russian-imposed revolution? There is something beautiful, something exciting about revolution. It has all the glitter of novelty, all the movement of insurrection. Human revolutions, surging up against imperfect human order, have as their archetype the first revolution, that of Satan against God. This is not to say that an established order may not also be Satanic, nor that no upheaval can be good, but precisely that the beauty of revolution, while real, is evilly real. The idolatry of revolution, though sinful, is in a sense creative: like Milton's Satan in *Paradise Lost*, the Moloch of revolution would shape a brilliant realm, full of fire and metallic beauty—but a realm of hatred and death, whose ruler has said, "Evil, be thou my good" (*Paradise Lost*, Book IV: 110f.).

The system of authoritarian repression, by contrast, is not an idol of the same kind, for it has no such cruel beauty, like Moloch, to enrapture its worshippers to throw their infants into its blazing belly. It is encrusted, lethargic, immobile, sluggish; it can hardly attract enthusiasts. It is more like the devil in Dante's *Inferno*, a blind and rigid being frozen forever in ice, where all motion, warmth and life have ceased forever—except the ceaseless grinding of three "revolutionaries" held in its jaws, its only sign of life! Dante's devil is ugly, not fascinating like Milton's. Authoritarian repression, like Dante's devil, is too ponderous, too ugly, too cold and dead to be an idol in the same way that revolution is. Thus it does not need the same kind of No. Against an encroaching evil power, one must speak the No of prohibition to stop it dead, lest it continue and conquer. Against lethargy and immobility, prohibitions are useless; against the deadly cold of Dante's hell, against the encroaching reign of ice, prohibition does no good. If revolution is fire, repression is ice. Both kill, but in different ways. This, and not any preferability of repression over revolution, is why the Christian should not launch the same No against repression. Against the encroaching ice, one must bring light and warmth in order to preserve life. This is another reason why mere no-saying, while necessary, is not enough.

The duty to say No to revolution so that there may be reformation involves the obligation to say Yes to reformation, and to work to bring it about. Otherwise we simply flee the fire of a revolutionary Moloch to be imprisoned in the perpetual ice of a different hell. Love and life can live near neither. In the present situation, in which the class struggle seems to be becoming universal, we must say No to revolution; not just a No of rigidity, but a No so that we can say Yes! to reformation. Reformation according to the Word of God, no less than revolution, but more health-fully, will melt the icy grip of existing evils. If present social structures manifest a bitter hostility to the Word of God (the Supreme Court decision against Bible-read-ing!), this means that to reform them according to that Word will involve some destructive work, just as a revolu-tion would. There will be places where the work of refor-mation will parallel that of revolution, and there are places where society's resistance to change will strike both the reformer *and* the revolutionary. The very similarity between their tasks and their enemies' makes a sharp Christian No to revolution all the more necessary. One cannot make common cause with any false messiah, even if only to build an *autobahn*; but to say only No would be to fail to follow the true Messiah, and to have neither the *autobahn* nor the straight way in the desert. The task of reformation is a positive task, demanding obedience, exertion and sacrifice. Only those who know the purpose of God, only the people of the Word, can consciously accomplish it; only reformation can lead man between the fire and the ice to a place where life and love can rule. The first work of reformation is to destroy the idols, to abandon dead works; the second is *immediately* to serve the living God. He is the only Ruler who loves His subjects and who will give them the inheritance of children.

8.

Reconciliation or Extortion?

In his dramatic confrontation with the prophets of Baal at Mount Carmel, Elijah challenged the indecisive Hebrews, "How long will you lean to both sides? If the Lord is God, follow Him; but if it is Baal, follow him." The account continues, "The people said nothing" (1 KINGS 18: 21).

In the spring of 1969, both the secular and the religious press were full of stories about demands for "reparations" to be paid by churches and synagogues to the American Negro. The original demands for $500,000,000 made in April 1969 had been upped to $3,000,000,000 by the end of the year and may still be rising. The demands were made by James Forman in the so-called Black Manifesto on behalf of the National Black Economic Development Council (NBEDC), until that time an unknown organization.[1] A number of prominent black Christians immediately denounced this Manifesto; Dr. Joseph H. Jackson, president of the National Baptist Convention, America's largest Negro denomination, called it "the same old Red manifesto painted black." By contrast, quite a number of the

[1] The Black Manifesto is reprinted in the *Congressional Record*, September 10, 1969.

white American churchmen to whom the Manifesto was addressed began to beat their breasts and look for ways to meet the demands.

The reaction of the major American denominational bodies to the Manifesto has not been uniform; it has varied from outright rejection by a few courageous Protestant bodies, Roman Catholics, and Jews, to submission and capitulation in various degrees by some of the major Protestant denominations, including the Protestant Episcopal Church and the United Presbyterian Church in the U.S.A. Europeans, whether Christian or not, are somewhat at a loss to understand how the demands of someone like Forman can be seriously entertained by sane church leaders. In the first place, it is not at all clear that he has any right to represent a significant body of American Negroes. His mandate seems to come only from himself—although after he received a respectful, even submissive, hearing from numerous denominational bodies and promises of massive "reparations," his stock in the black community went up. Thus we have a paradoxical situation in which a spokesman who is not commissioned by his people, nor even acceptable to large numbers of them, and who roundly denounces Christian institutions and promises to destroy them, derives his recognition from the respectful hearing given him by Christian institutions. It is also worth noting that the acceptance which Forman and other extremists have received from American church leaders has led some Europeans to think that the churches must in fact be guiltier than they would otherwise have supposed!

Why should a book devoted to the sweeping, worldwide topic of Christianity and the class struggle give space to the consideration of a phenomenon as isolated and eccentric-seeming as that of the Forman demands and the churches' reactions to them? The answer is simple. The

very effrontery of the demands, or rather the supine manner in which many of the major churches have reacted to
them, reveals two things of prime importance for the future
of organized Christianity in the United States:

(1) The officials and administrators of a number of
churches have taken leave not merely of Christian orthodoxy as a criterion for religious judgments, but also of
reason and common sense for practical ones.

(2) Great numbers of church leaders despair of being
able to do anything effective to meet the conditions out
of which Forman's demands arose. In other words, they
have so little imagination, energy, and willingness to bring
to bear on the problem that they will consider any price,
even the most absurd, if it only appears to get them off the
hook of moral responsibility.

The tragic thing about this abandonment both of reason
and of initiative is that accepting demands like those of
the Black Manifesto only gives irresponsible and fanatical
people the financial power with which to make a bad situation desperate. In other words, the churches seem, by
their reactions, to show that they no longer possess the
power of reason or of discernment, and very probably the
small remnant of rationality they do possess is smothered
by their guilty consciences concerning what they have
failed to do in the past, before the underprivileged began
demanding instead of pleading. We should also note that
in this matter, as in many other questions (e.g., the question of diplomatic recognition for Communist China),
denominational leaders show very little respect for the
wishes of the majority of church members, and indeed very
little for the members themselves. (The fact that their
decisions are frequently quite contrary to the wishes of the
church members is clear; their disdain for the "silent majority" in the churches is evident from the fact that the

leaders are making very little attempt to *persuade* their followers that these unpopular decisions are morally right.) Many congregations have refused to contribute to denominational budgets that include large sums for organizations like the NBEDC. The usual reaction of denominational officials has been to condemn such reluctant congregations and individuals for selfishness and racism, not to try to show them why they think that the contributions are necessary. This authoritarian and arrogant attitude, "the public be damned," may result from an inward awareness in such officials that it is likely to be very hard to justify the payment of "reparations," particularly to the people who have been demanding them, in terms either of Christian theology or of common sense.

Before we can go on to discuss the positive challenge of the reformation of society, then, we must examine the mentality which prevails in our churches, and indeed throughout much of the "Christian" West, and which is most glaringly revealed in the churches' acquiescence in the demands for "reparations." From this extreme phenomenon, and our reaction to it, we will be able to read the measure of our competence to understand and our willingness to face the larger problems of which it is a symptom. If churches and their leaders cannot reach a common-sense, Christianly sound decision in so transparently clear a situation, there is little hope they will discover the principles necessary to resolve issues that are more basic and at the same time more difficult.

CONFUSION

It is difficult to understand what can have motivated the commissioners of the United Presbyterian Church at San Antonio in the spring of 1969, when they invited James Forman to address their assembly, or all the other churchmen who have so willingly swallowed both the concept of reparations and Forman's assumed right to speak on behalf of all Negro Americans. Apparently their guilt feelings have been so overstimulated that their critical faculties and their wills are paralyzed. The doctrine of collective guilt, which Hitler applied to the Jews and which the victorious Allies, with some reservations, applied to the Germans, we have now turned upon ourselves. Is a president assassinated? We are all guilty. Are there rioting and arson in the "ghetto"? They are the fault of the prosperous suburbs. Does a juvenile assault an old woman? Society is at fault. And so on. Are the Negroes dissatisfied? It is because the Caucasian majority has oppressed them. Are they violent? It is because we resist their just demands. Do they threaten to subjugate the majority? It only serves us right.

At least three things have to be observed about this line of thought:

(1) To accept the Black Manifesto as valid in any sense, other than a valid expression of untrue, irrational, and destructive convictions, is a demonstration that one's mind has been stupefied. It states, "Christianity was used to help enslave us," calls for "total disruption of selected church sponsoring agencies," and adds, "we will have to declare war on the white Christian churches and synagogues . . ." It is also evident, although not explicitly stated, that the Black Manifesto requires the repudiation of the Christian faith by Negroes. The only sane reaction that a church with any respect for Christ, the Gospels, and its own calling can make to such a tirade is to say, "You are beside yourselves." The churches may well confess to having failed the Negro, to having in effect condoned his exploitation, to having sinned against him. One can even accept the Black Manifesto as a cry of rage that to some extent was provoked by these failures. But to accept it as *legitimate*, is to betray Christ, to betray human reason, and last—but far from

least—to betray all of the black Christians who have accepted Christ as their Lord. What are they to think when a Forman announces that Christianity is a vehicle of enslavement and white Christian churchmen piously mutter their agreement?

(2) The line, "We are all guilty," is not merely a form of auto-paralysis; it is also false, both on Christian and on common-sense terms. The Christian faith knows individual responsibility and human solidarity ("For all have sinned," writes St. Paul, "and come short of the glory of God," ROMANS 3:23). It does not recognize *racial* guilt, except in the sense that the people of God are doubly accountable *to Him* for their misdoings (AMOS 3:2). Common sense tells us that if everyone is guilty, then no one is guilty, that is, no one is personally responsible. If there was ever a broadly based phenomenon of maltreatment of one people by another, it was that of the Jews by the Germans, and yet we rightly (if not always accurately) attempted to identify and apprehend the individual Germans who were responsible (that is, *answerable*) for those crimes. No doubt one of the reasons for the orgy of journalistic and professorial breast-beating when President Kennedy was murdered ("We are all guilty"; "The climate of hate is responsible"; and so on) was apprehension lest some embarrassingly specific individual or conspiracy should turn out to have been behind it. (For example, had it really been shown that the Cuban government was behind the conspiracy, it might well have been a second Sarajevo.) And of course if "we white Americans" are all guilty of exploitation of the Negroes, is there nothing that "all we blacks" are guilty of against the Caucasian majority? One acquaintance, when he first heard of the reparations demand, said, "Pay them, of course—just deduct them from all the wages paid for work that was never done." The black

militant who cries, "We made this country rich with our exploited labor," calls for the reply from the white reactionary, "*We* made it rich despite all your shiftlessness!" There is probably a measure of truth in both charges, but there is peace in neither. Only God can assign the blame and punish the guilty, the majority of whom, being long dead, have already gone to meet Him. Our task is not to inflict or to solicit punishment, but to build.

(3) Finally, to accede to such demands is irrational because the very words of the Manifesto make it clear that the money received will be used to exacerbate the situation, to promote hatred and violence. The logistics of the white-black relationship in the United States, however, indicate that if the blacks succeed in unchaining real, widespread violence, they will destroy themselves. How can white churchmen encourage and abet Negroes in pursuing a course that, humanly speaking, can only end in their destruction? Unless we assume that there are some among them who would willingly sacrifice the Negroes of America in a bloody race war, perhaps in order to weaken the United States as a whole or to transform society in some direction, we must conclude that the white churchmen are so preoccupied with their own guilt that they are unable to think about the needs of others. It is rather as though someone were to rush into a sporting-goods store demanding to be given a gun with which to avenge himself against the U.S. Army. To yield to his demand is in effect to consent to his suicide. One may do it out of fear, but one can hardly call it an exercise of Christian responsibility.

EXTORTION

The demands of the NBEDC differ from that of the man in the sporting-goods store in that the Black Manifesto wants the gun to use it on the man providing it. When someone demands money from you, threatening immediate violence, it is robbery; if the threats are for some future time, it is extortion. When someone demands money now so that he can equip himself to do you violence later, it is hard to imagine what to call it. Few major church observers have seen as clearly as the evangelical fortnightly *Christianity Today*, which referred to it quite frankly as a shakedown.[2] It is, in fact, extortion with a remarkable refinement.

In ordinary extortion, the extortioner demands that his victim give him something, otherwise he will take everything; in the refinement seen at San Antonio and elsewhere, the extortioner demands something now so that he can take everything later. In other words, to yield today is to ask for more trouble tomorrow. The craven submission of church leaders to such demands not only reveals a lack of self-respect and of a sense of the dignity of the church, but also exhibits a kind of contempt for the Negro claimants. Apparently no matter what the Negro militants threaten, their white victims do not take them seriously, do not credit them with enough determination to carry out their threats. Otherwise, how could they put into their hands the weapons with which to "wage war against the white Christian churches and synagogues"? People who accept such demands deserve nothing better than to be exploited.

The tragic thing about highly placed churchmen who submit to extortion is that they thereby abdicate any possibility of exercising spiritual and moral leadership to calm down the racial crisis. Certainly no black militant will respect the moral qualities of a man who caves in before his rhetoric; the church members, whose money is being

[2] James M. Boice, "Shakedown in San Antonio," *Christianity Today*, June 6, 1969, p. 836.

handed over to meet the demands, will hardly respect him more. The leaders may claim that they, like Chamberlain, are buying "peace in our time," but many of their parishioners will quickly recognize that they in fact are buying unreason, mutual contempt, and hatred. Fearful submission to demands cannot be masked either as generosity or as Christian charity, and surely no one is going to look on it as the exercise of *leadership*.

"No Charity." One of the strangely perverse slogans of our day is, "We want justice, not charity!" The idea seems to be that the giving of charity somehow enables the giver to exalt himself, while to receive it is demeaning. This concept is quite alarming even on merely humanistic terms: if we never accepted anything we had not earned or could not pay for, none of us would have survived infancy; and apart from infancy, many of us would have met disaster in other situations beyond our own control.[3] From the Christian perspective, we would have no hope at all apart from the charity (*agape*) of God, for if He gave us the reward we merit, we would all be lost. We cannot *merit* His love, but we can and should reflect it and exhibit it to others. Those who say, "We don't want charity," are in fact saying a dreadful thing. Extortion is not charity, and it is not justice either. One aspect of the extortion-submission technique in interracial relationships is that it is sure to blight all chances for love: no one loves an extortioner, and no extortioner loves his victim.

We cannot expect the alienated, enraged, frustrated Negroes like Forman to approach the churches in a spirit of love, but we should expect the liberal churchmen who

[3] Professor Jacques Ellul of the Faculty of Law at the University of Bordeaux, France, analyzes this perverse slogan in his *Exégèse des nouveaux lieux communs* (Paris: Calmann-Lévy, 1966; Eng. translation, *A Critique of the New Commonplaces*, New York: Knopf, 1967).

talk so much about love not to take actions dictated by hate on one side and fear on the other. Many such churchmen have had a great deal to say about how love requires the courage to take unpopular action, to stand up to abuse, etc., but they grow strangely meek when confronted with the demands of demagogues who are not amenable to reason. Certainly the failure to say No to even the most outrageous and palpably absurd demands can only increase the arrogance of the extremists and undercut the attempts of black moderates to preserve elementary considerations of reason, justice, and charity. In short, those "Christians" who submit, on behalf of their churches, to demands like those of the Black Manifesto not only capitulate to unreason and make a travesty of justice; they also destroy every possibility that *love* will influence interracial relations.

This kind of extortion, if carried out, provides the extortioners with the necessary means to complete the subjugation of their victims. For a parallel to this remarkable phenomenon, we have to look long in the pages of history. The Byzantine Empire, which succeeded the Roman Empire, for a time followed the policy of buying off the barbarians with substantial cash payments, reasoning that to do so was less dangerous and cheaper than going to war. It worked for a while—until the Empire began to run out of easy money and the barbarians began pounding on the gates of Constantinople. Barbarians, incidentally, are not necessarily people who have had no opportunity to learn civilization—they are sometimes people who reject the disciplines of civilization as too hard, and as unnecessary. After all, if one can frighten the civilized people into turning over to the barbarians the fruits of their labors, why learn to work? Demands of the Forman kind are certainly barbaric in this sense: it is significant that the concept of "black capitalism," which would involve creativity and productive work, is specifically rejected in favor of exploiting those who have been working all along.

All this is not to deny that there is a measure of plausibility in the concept of "reparations." There has been economic exploitation of the Negro in American history. But if some extent of the "damages" were to be calculated, who has standing to receive them? Because Negro slaves had to work under degrading conditions and without pay in the ante-bellum South, does this entitle their descendants to receive pay without working today? Since the vast majority of Americans have ancestors who were underprivileged and exploited in Europe or North America in the past, they too could claim reparations. And what about the Irish-Americans who, while suffering discrimination themselves, provided so many of the Union troops who won freedom for the black slaves?

It may be relevant to point out that the concept of reparations has an unfortunate history. Germany demanded reparations from France after the Franco-Prussian War, and the political and economic results were such that Bismarck remarked that if he had it to do again, he would force France to accept reparations from Germany. Among the many unjust features of the 1919 Versailles Treaty were clauses requiring Germany to pay astronomical sums as reparations. The reparations contributed not only to the German sense of unjust treatment, but also to the inflation which ruined the German middle class, destroyed the stability of the social order, and paved the way for the rise of Hitler.

Injury done to a slave in the nineteenth century cannot be made good by a reparations payment to a twentieth-century descendant. The only real atonement for a society based on exploitation and arrogance would be the building of a society of justice and love, and this is precisely what the extortion of reparations would prevent. If Americans have a guilty conscience about the sins of their fathers in maintaining an unjust society, they should have the clarity and the courage to recognize that submitting to a shake-down is not the same thing as establishing justice.

THE DARKENED MIND

We have already touched upon the fact that exaggerated guilt feelings cloud the minds and numb the wills of countless white Americans vis-à-vis the question of Negro rights, so that they have neither the perspicacity to see nor the courage to say that two wrongs do not make a right. The artificial stimulation of guilt feelings is a favorite device of many who expect to gain more from an emotional rather than a rational response to their demands. For example, when John F. Kennedy was assassinated, there was a great deal of agitation about firearms ownership in the United States, and the murder of Robert Kennedy and of Dr. Martin Luther King led to hysterical and largely successful campaigns to destroy the rights guaranteed in the Second Amendment. Very little attention was desired for the *facts* of the case, which might have been quite detrimental to the new legislation, and the facts were largely submerged in public breast-beatings about, "We are all guilty," "a society of violence," and so on *ad nauseam*. A book published in 1969 has brought light to bear on the question, but unfortunately the wave of guilt has largely accomplished its work.[4]

An even more flagrant example of this technique was the nationwide orgy of guilt feelings that resulted from the spectacular worldwide publicity given to the Songmy

[4] Bill R. Davidson, *To Keep and Bear Arms* (New Rochelle, N.Y.: Arlington House, 1969).

massacre or alleged massacre, beginning conveniently at about the time of the November 1969 "Moratorium." Surely reason would dictate that no massacre of civilians by U.S. troops, whatever the circumstances, could in itself destroy the material and moral reasons for the United States' presence in Vietnam. No one suggests that the deliberate slaughter of German civilian populations by the R.A.F. and to a lesser extent by the U.S.A.A.F., or of Japanese by the A.A.F. annulled the necessity of fighting and defeating Nazi Germany and imperial Japan. Those air raids were matters of policy decided at the highest level, whereas no one has claimed that the massacre at Songmy, whatever the facts, expressed either U.S. Army or government policy. Yet the Songmy affair was seized upon by a large segment of the news media as a marvelous way to arouse guilt feelings and to destroy rational thought on a more important issue.

Another example, more to the point of our present concern, is the often repeated arguments that looting, arson, and even murder, such as took place in the Watts, Detroit, Newark, and Washington riots, must be, if not excused, at least endured on the grounds of injustices done in the past to those responsible. Quite apart from the fact that very few of the rioters had *themselves* suffered serious injustices, the argument proves too much and excuses everything. For the Germans had in fact suffered some exploitation after 1918 at the hands of Jews; the Palestinian Arabs of today can say the same thing; it is probable that *no* act of racial or national violence takes place against entirely innocent victims, if only for the reason that no entirely innocent individuals, or races, or nations, exist.

The reason why real and imagined guilt can be used with such success to paralyze the reason and will of large segments of the population—or at least of the intelligentsia

—is two-fold. (We must observe that the general population is far less sensitive either to guilt feelings or to media exploitation of them than are the intellectuals, despite strenuous attempts to sensitize it.) First, the ability to think critically, to recognize contradictions, and to make clear distinctions is not cultivated in the American educational system.* Second, there is an almost total rejection of absolute and objective standards whereby actions and ideas may be evaluated. The first reason means that almost no one is capable—to continue with the example we have been using—of seeing the implications of the Black Manifesto. Plenty of people do not like it and recognize its explicit threat to the United States, but very few are capable of seeing its implications. Thus people who oppose giving money to the NBEDC can easily be made to feel guilty of selfishness and of racial bigotry, when a little critical thinking would show them that refusal is required by concern for the Negro and that submission, not refusal, will increase bigotry. The second reason means that nothing can be judged as good or bad in itself. Thus it happens that a church, which is supposed to regard itself as the body of Christ against which even the gates of hell shall not prevail (MATTHEW 16:18), applauds on hearing threats to "make war on white Christian churches." This is definitely false

* For example, in the 1964 presidential battle Senator Goldwater proposed making Social Security coverage voluntary. Governor Rockefeller of New York charged that this would be a "national tragedy." Most of the news media applauded Rockefeller for rushing to the rescue of the common man, thus threatened with tragedy by Goldwater's heartless suggestion. Let us not go into the relative merits and disadvantages of Goldwater's proposal; let us only observe that Rockefeller's "national tragedy" takes it for granted that the vast majority of the common people are too foolish, selfish, or improvident to make provision for their future unless forced to do so. This may conceivably be true, but the implication is not very flattering to the voters. Very few of them saw this; most were indignant at Goldwater and grateful to Rockefeller for his generous defense of their interests.

Christianity, by which a number of blind leaders think to make peace with the gods of this world. As Jacques Ellul points out:

That the acceptance of condemnation can be a sign of humility, the chance to establish a dialogue, or a trial of our faith willed by God, is true, but it in no wise implies that the persecutors of the church are in the right! Let us consider the Chaldaean: he is God's agent for the chastisement of Israel, and he is so proclaimed and described by the prophet *to the people of God*. But at the same time, the prophet announces his condemnation and ruin, precisely for having acted against what is *nevertheless* the people of God (ISAIAH 10:5ff.; JEREMIAH, chapters 25 and 50). The Chaldaean is in no wise justified for being what he is because of the disobedience of Israel, and so it is today![5]

What has happened to permit churchmen to do exactly the opposite of what their professed loyalties require, and to cause laymen to approve of these men, or at least not to challenge them? Unfortunately, the phenomenon is not limited to the Christian church, although it is at its most intense there. We have drawn attention to the way in

---

[5] Jacques Ellul, *Fausse présence au monde moderne* [False Presence in the Modern World] (Paris: Les Bergers et les Mages, 1963), p. 34. Unfortunately, French Protestants do not think more clearly than their American brethren, for Ellul continues: "However, quite the contrary, we see Christians joyfully acclaiming everything which is an attack against Christianity and the church: 'Mme de B. tells us that Christianity is a viscous hypocrisy? But how right she is! Psychiatrists explain that faith is only a substitute for repressed sexual impulses? How well-said! A government expels the Christians, imprisons the bishops, tortures the priests? What good luck! Finally there will be an end to compromise, and it proves that the church was allied to the capitalists. The government wants to suppress Christian schools? Fine, that is doing us a favor (so the Hungarian church in 1955, when the government suppressed one theological faculty out of three).' And you belong to the party which openly proclaims its anti-Christian policies, etc. . . . Everything which drags the Christian faith into the mud and tends to suppress the church is received with joy." *Ibid.*, pp. 34f.

which universities are becoming the strongholds of un-scientific, anti-intellectual, and authoritarian movements, which they harbor and sometimes even encourage in the name of academic liberty. When Bertrand Russell died, all the Swiss newspapers eulogized him as "a champion of peace." It was Russell who popularized the slogan, "Better Red than dead!" Every Swiss man, including newspaper writers and editors, spends a good bit of his life in the Swiss army, based on the principle that it would be better to fight than to lose freedom—and yet Russell is acclaimed. Examples could be multiplied *ad infinitum*.

Some people believe that the human mind itself is under attack. According to Francis A. Schaeffer, when the West began to abandon the Christian framework, it lost not only its values but also its ability to think, and events would seem to bear him out. Philosopher Herman Dooyeweerd believes that the Western mind is entering a twilight zone in which it will be incapable of ordinary logic and reason.[6] The phenomenon of drug use among so-called intellectuals attests the growing willingness to abandon reason and its laws.

For the thinking Christian, the abandonment of funda-mental biblical principles is not merely a moral and religious catastrophe, that is, a flight from Christianity, but an intellectual one as well, that is, a flight from reason. Evidence of this appears in the fact that this intellectual catastrophe is most pronounced precisely in the church, which was and should be most dependent upon biblical principles of judgment and action. What would have happened if Forman had presented his claims to a secular institution like Harvard University, which has over one billion dollars in assets, and which could actually have

[6] Francis A. Schaeffer, *Escape from Reason* (London and Chicago: Inter-Varsity, 1968); Herman Dooyeweerd, *In the Twilight of Western Thought*, 2nd ed. (Nutley, N.J.: Craig, 1965).

paid Forman's original "reparations" bill? There the vestiges
of reason are somewhat stronger. Harvard would not have
accorded him the gullible attention of the Presbyterians in
San Antonio and of other prominent churchmen elsewhere.
But Harvard too is engaged in a withdrawal, if not a
precipitous flight from reason, more slowly but equally
definitely.

When Christians abandon biblical principles for human
traditions, the results are not merely non-Christian, but
nonsense. In a society built upon the basis of a Christian
tradition of thought, the loss of Christian values will
quickly paralyze and befuddle Christian institutions like
the church, and eventually even secular ones like the
university. Biblical values are not merely superstructure;
they are part of the intellectual foundation as well. Of
course, they could be replaced by another set of values—
communism has done this to some extent where it rules—
but where they are merely allowed to erode, and are not
replaced, their loss brings on a paralysis of the mind, not
merely of the moral and religious sense. Only the convinced Christian will say that biblical values are absolute,
and ought to be preserved, but anyone can recognize the
evident fact that if they are abandoned and nothing
definite and coherent replaces them, chaos results. Even
the pragmatic *modus vivendi* of twentieth-century Western
secularists is more dependent on the Christian base than
they recognize, as the incipient intellectual chaos shows.
The intellectual traditions of the Enlightenment, developed
in opposition to orthodox Christian thought, are still dependent on it and are not strong enough to survive a real
collapse of the Christian consensus. This is the theoretical
background; the practical results are seen in the fact that
intelligent people submit to extortion demands and think
that thereby they are doing a good work.

The leaders of the United Presbyterians (along with

many others) have become precisely what Jesus called the Pharisees who abandoned the Word of God, blind leaders of the blind, and not merely in religious matters, but even in practical ones (cf. MATTHEW 15:1–20). There is a kind of bitter irony in the situation. Only two years after the United Presbyterian Church had downgraded the scripturally sound *Westminster Confession of Faith* to replace it with the *Confession of 1967*, which puts so much emphasis on human reconciliation, the church found itself, in its 1969 San Antonio assembly,[7] agreeing to extortioners' demands that are going to spell an end to sentiments of reconciliation on all sides. What a spectacle it was to see the learned commissioners gravely entertain demands that, in effect, said, "Because we plan to despoil you of everything soon, therefore give us something now." In His debate with the Pharisees, Jesus quoted the prophet Isaiah on replacing commandments of God with commandments of men. The prophet went on to warn of the consequences, "The wisdom of their wise men shall perish, and the discernment of their discerning men shall be hid" (ISAIAH 29:14). What more appropriate words could be found to epitomize the collapse of reason and the will before demands such as those made by the Forman group? Wisdom has perished, and discernment is hid!

RECONCILIATION

It may seem unnecessary to expatiate at such length on one particular phase of the race-class struggle, but it is important. It is important because this almost ludicrous situation so clearly demonstrates something that, although it is always true, is not always so evident. The will of God calls for reconciliation. Abandoning this divine imperative

[7] See fn. 2 above.

for the sake of a prudent, "expedient" submission to pressure ("Peace in our time"?) is a foolish course which will destroy those who follow it. Disregard for biblical principles always brings eventual trouble, but here the impending trouble is so obviously built into this disregard that failure to see it coming can only be a result of the fulfillment of the warning, "the wisdom of their wise men shall perish." You can only think that extortion will bring reconciliation if in fact you cannot think.

Today the churches must choose between working for reconciliation in human society in obedience to the will of God and yielding to extortion in submission to the demands of men. The two cannot be combined. To submit to extortion cannot be a preliminary to reconciliation, for the extortioner will learn to despise his victim just as the victim will come to hate his exploiter. The chances for reconciliation among adversaries are good when each can respect the humanity and the integrity of the other, but this is never possible in the case of extortion. An armed robber who knows he has used *force majeure* on his victim does not have to despise him, but an extortioner who knows that his victim has cringed at his threats and has been paralyzed by his own guilt feelings can hardly help but despise him. To yield to the demands of a Forman is not to give the Negro community evidence of one's reasonableness and interest in reconciliation; it is to demonstrate one's weakness in thought and action. It can only increase the disillusionment of the moderates and the arrogance of the extremists, and prepare the day when the affronts will become intolerable and open violence will be the desperate answer to new demands.

The churches of America should be grateful to Mr. Forman and to his National Black Economic Development Council. He could have presented his demands in another fashion, in one which would have made them less obviously a shakedown. He could have said to the churches, "If you will show your goodwill and your desire to atone for conscious and unconscious wrongs done to black people in the past, we will do all in our power for reconciliation." That would have been a proposal to which the churches would have been morally obliged to listen. Instead, he said, "Give us something now and know that we intend to take everything later!" By so doing, he unmasked his extortion for what it is, a preliminary to "total control." Curiously enough, he also unmasked the intellectual and moral poverty of those he approached.

The irony of the situation is that submission to such demands is precisely *not* the way of love, of reconciliation among the races; it is the way of hatred and real violence. To yield on such an issue will not impress the black extremists with the virtue and reasonableness of their white "reparations"-payers, but will convince them of their victims' weakness and suitability for further exactions and indignities. Success attracts, and the reasonable men, even black Christians, who have opposed such extortion, will find it progressively harder not to take advantage of such willing victims. The white "contributors," meanwhile, will grow more and more restive under the combination of increasing exactions and growing contempt; ultimately violence will become inevitable. That, in the last analysis, can help no one, least of all the Negroes, who do constitute, in fact, only 10 percent of the American population, and who are also very vulnerable to violence in their turn.

To agree to extortion is neither reasonable nor loving. It will bring violence and hatred, not harmony and love. In such a case, the courage to resist it is not merely more honorable than complaisance, it is also ultimately safer. The churches of America have been confronted, in the Black

Maniresto, with a compelling challenge, no less compelling than that with which the prophet Elijah confronted the Hebrews. Forman, unlike Elijah, has not come with the Word of the Lord. He has come, wittingly or not, with the word of the diabolos, but the need to choose and not hesitate is equally great. To hesitate, or to choose wrongly, is not merely to *court* disaster, but—as far as human predictions can go—to *guarantee* it. Both white and black Americans can be grateful to Mr. Forman for this: he has presented his demands in such a manner as to make the dictates of conscience and expediency coincide. The Christian answer is that God commands reconciliation, not capitulation; reason also forbids extortion, for it never ends, except in violence.

Confronted with demands that are tantamount to extortion, the white Christian must answer with a clear, calm, and courageous No. Only thus can he hope to keep his self-respect and to regain the respect of the black man, without which reconciliation is impossible. Yet he may not stop with a mere self-protective No. To do so would be to disobey Christ's commandments to love and to give of oneself and of one's substance. But first things first: first the No! to the demands of the diabolos, then the Yes! to the commands of Christ. For reconciliation, no effort is unreasonable, no sacrifice wasted; for extortion, nothing is reasonable, and all is wasted. It is deeply Christian, and deeply practical, to paraphrase the revolutionary slogan and to say, "Millions for reconciliation, but not one penny for extortion!" And not merely to say it, but to do it: refuse the penny, *but spend the millions.*

9.

America's Babylonian Captivity

WHEN the army of the Assyrian King Sennacherib laid siege to Jerusalem, his commander promised the inhabitants that if they would surrender, he would lead them away to "a land of grain and wine, a land of food and vineyards, a land of olive oil and honey, where you may live and not die" (II KINGS 18:32). But Jerusalem did not surrender and Sennacherib's mighty army was destroyed by God. A century later Jerusalem was again under siege, this time by the army of the Neo-Babylonian monarch Nebuchadnezzar, and this time it fell, and the Jews were taken captive to Babylon. There we find that their lot was not so hard, for members of them rose to wealth and prominence. Apparently life in the political and economic center of a great empire was to the liking of many, for when Cyrus of Persia released the captives, only 42,300 were willing to go back to Israel. The rest preferred life in Babylon and the other great and wealthy cities of the new Persian Empire to the hard work of reconstruction back in Israel.

It is obviously more appealing, more challenging, more productive, more "efficient" to remain near the center of political and economic power than to be off in a distant and ruined province trying to rebuild tumbled-down walls and competing with the jackals and a hostile population of squatters. Yet it was the Jews who returned to Israel under Zerubbabel, Ezra, and Nehemiah, rather than the multitude who chose prosperity in Babylonia, who have left their mark upon history, and through whom the Messiah was born. In a modern analogy, there are many Jews, refugees and others, who have won fame and fortune in Europe and America since World War II, but it is those who have gone to Israel, to hardship and war, who will leave their mark on the history of the twentieth century.

Twentieth-century America (and much of Europe) is to many of its citizens, and especially for the Christians, what Babylon was to the Jews. The Christian of any age, like the Jew in Babylon, is supposed to know that he is a stranger and a pilgrim on the earth (HEBREWS 11:13), and to prefer that his hand forget its skill than that he forget the City of God (PSALM 137:5). But the City of Man is so broad and fair! Dietrich Bonhoeffer, John A. T. Robinson, Harvey E. Cox, and many others have sung the praises of "man come of age," of the "secular city." (The Swedish translation of Cox's *Secular City* has as its title the rhetorical question, "Did God Create the Metropolis?") And so the "city of man" is built, with its hanging gardens, its perfumed palaces, and its Mene, Tekel on the wall.

Within this city, the Christians prosper, sharing, like all the others—or most of them—in the glut of consumer goods, fancy foods, luxuries, second homes, European vacations, and all the other bounty of technology and industry. It is true, of course, that two thirds of the world's population lives in poverty and often in hunger; that a very large number of nations have laws that make slaves of all their people (see above, chapter three); and all this with remarkably little attention from the architects and advertisers of the flourishing City of Man. Instead, the city hardly built, they devote themselves to encouraging the barbarization of an underprivileged racial minority and the indolence and hedonism of the young and not-so-young heirs of the city's opulence.

Only ten years ago, when John F. Kennedy was inaugurated into the office of President of the United States, he warned, "We are in danger of losing something solid at the core. We are losing that Pilgrim and pioneer spirit of initiative and independence—that old-fashioned Spartan devotion to duty, honor, and country." Today his warning has been largely fulfilled. We are in the throes of what the *Christian Century* calls the "soft revolution" and Lunn and Lean call "the cult of softness."[1] If something solid is missing, we are told, we are better off without it. There is something terribly tragic—and even diabolical—about the cult of self-indulgence that is becoming general in Western nations, especially in the United States, just at a time when the challenges to work and to sacrifice seem greatest. Is it not very strange that the same people are advocating massive help for the underprivileged, underdeveloped, undernourished in the United States and around the world, and at the same time proclaiming a cult of softness that encourages people to put self above service and indulgence above industry? Who is to provide the food, the medical supplies, the industrial goods to battle poverty around the world if the wealthy countries of the West spend their riches and their energy in the quest for entertainment, leisure, and pleasure?

There is something not merely paradoxical but tragic in the way in which many members of the student generation,

[1] Sam Keen, "The 'Soft' Revolution Explored," *Christian Century*, December 31, 1969, pp. 1667ff.; Sir Arnold Lunn and Garth Lean, *The Cult of Softness* (London: Blandford, 1965).

supposedly rebelling against the hypocrisy and selfishness of their elders, demand freedom and power for themselves— only to use it, for the most part, to indulge themselves and to evade work and responsibility. In the fall of 1969, the Swiss paper *La Tribune* carried two ecstatic articles on the hippy pilgrimage to Katmandu. During the week following the second article, the Paris *Figaro* reported on the same migration, but said that the real adventure was that of the French youths who were giving several years of their lives in self-sacrificial work in the Indian villages.[2] Nevertheless, the "adventure" of the hippies retains media attention, while the self-sacrificial labors of young missionaries, Peace Corps workers, teachers, engineers and others receive attention only when someone creates a scandal.

Thus at the very moment when all our analyses tell us that there is an unparalleled need for unselfish service around the world, and when our young people are discovering ever more frantic ways of rebelling against or dropping out of our materialistic society, very few are willing to see the obvious answer: this wealth, energy, and productivity, which we now know cannot satisfy our deepest needs, could be channeled into the service of those whose *most elementary needs* have yet been met, and thus go far towards filling our own moral and spiritual vacuum.

BY THE WATERS OF BABYLON

Unfortunately, many of the same people who decry the luxury, selfishness, and insensitivity of materialistic society nevertheless want to remain well within reach of its com-

[2] *La Tribune* (Lausanne), September 28 and October 5, 1969; *Le Figaro*, October 10, 1969.

forts. Just as most of the Jews before the time of Cyrus wept when they remembered Jerusalem, but nevertheless, when the Great King gave them permission to return, *stayed in Babylon*, so it is true that across the board in our wealthy society even its critics are themselves all too eager to enjoy all its privileges and are seldom willing to deprive themselves for the sake of any ideal.

The United States, like a number of only slightly less wealthy European societies, seems to be on a kind of protracted Belshazzar's feast, which goes on and on, even while the "northern barbarians" are completing their careful plans for conquest. The picture of life in the United States given to foreign readers by the international editions of *Time*, *Life*, and *Newsweek*, as well as by other widely circulated publications, is one of a society sated with self-indulgence and absolutely indifferent to suffering near and far.

On the one hand, it must be said that the *Time-Life-Newsweek* picture of a degenerate, violent, corrupt America does an injustice to a great majority of the American people, many of whom still have "something solid at the core." Nevertheless, if the picture is not accurate as news, it is a kind of self-fulfilling prophecy, for the media create the kind of life they describe. On the other hand, then, this distortion that is presented as reality and taken for reality around the world is becoming reality with alarming speed.

The critics of American society and of capitalist, industrial, technological society in general are like those Jews who preferred to sing of Zion in Babylon rather than return to Israel. With some exceptions, the critics and their heroes live off the fruits of capitalism, often enough off unearned income. Even the vaunted "communes" and rural settlements can exist only because a combination of factors permits them to obtain or use the land and insulates them from the normal consequences of inefficiency, lack of skill, laziness, and the misfortunes that are common to all men. Perhaps the most spectacular travesty is the almost instantaneous metamorphosis of Daniel Cohn-Bendit, hero of the attempted Paris May revolution of 1968, into a high-living movie producer; but a similarly self-indulgent opportunism can be seen in many other places. The ample salaries of the most violent academic critics of our materialistic society are paid by the state or by private endowments, and it is seldom that they renounce the *money*, although often enough they denounce the "selfishness and hypocrisy" of those who provide it.

But Babylon the Great fell, and its comfortable critics with it. The little band of Jews who returned to Israel has left a far deeper mark on history than all the great rulers and rich merchants of the Babylonian and Persian Empires. There was no *need* for Babylon to fall to the Medes and the Persians, and no *need* for Persia to succumb to the small army of Alexander the Great. But life by the waters of Babylon had so enervated the leaders of those empires that—to paraphrase John F. Kennedy—there was nothing solid at the core.

In recent months many major news media, including publications as diverse as *Newsweek* and *U.S. News and World Report*, have devoted major coverage to "middle America," the "silent majority." Depending on the perspective and prejudices of the publication in question, the "silent majority" may be presented sympathetically or sarcastically, but one feature recurs again and again: the majority is troubled, dissatisfied, frustrated. It feels sorry for itself. The blacks, the students, the hippies get all the attention, all the money; the "silent majority" does all the work, pays all the taxes, and must chase after its dreams of consumer happiness with shrinking dollars. While the older

adults strive to provide their families with split-level hous-
ing, color television, several cars, boats, vacations, etc., they
grow constantly more frustrated at their failure to retain
the respect of their children or to gain contentment themselves.

Is it not the perfect paradigm of the warning given by
Jesus: "For whosoever will save his life shall lose it . . . for
what shall it profit a man, if he shall gain the whole world,
and suffer the loss of his soul?" (Mark 8: 35–36)? The loss
of "something solid at the core" is more serious than even
John F. Kennedy feared; it is the loss of the soul, for individuals and for society.

THE RUINED PLACES OF ZION

Criticism alone is no answer. Imperial Rome at its most
corrupt was not lacking in bitter critics. The epigrammatist
Martial (circa A.D. 40–102) made his disgust with the vices
of Rome abundantly clear, but he also made it abundantly
clear that he was participating in them and profiting by
them. In like manner, we may suspect that when a *Life*
editor bemoans the materialism of twentieth-century America, it does not mean that he has renounced it himself,
or even its grosser features. To identify an evil does not
necessarily imply that one breaks with it, alas! The "new
cult of the occult" has been *identified* by our great media,
and also *promoted* by them.

Something more than criticism is needed, and that
something is action. There is no cure for the frustrating
and degrading preoccupation with oneself, one's needs,
and one's comfort, other than to begin taking thought for
others. The circulation of several U.S. magazines in other
countries has been mentioned above. Perhaps no single
thing is so damaging to the American image abroad as the

picture they give of a population swimming in abundance, yet constantly sniveling about inflation and taxes and slobbering after new luxuries and pleasures it cannot yet have. But it is not the degrading effect such presentations have on America's image that should be our chief concern, but the deadening effect they have on America's people.

Life in Babylon is sweet, perhaps; but too sweet—it is sickening. What is needed is a new return to Zion, a pioneering venture, a determined attempt to build up the waste places, the waste places that are so prevalent in our own society and around the world.

Against the problems of American society, our *imperatores* and *optimates*, our presidents and greatest families, have launched ambitious programs. Money has been poured into education, urban renewal, medical and social security, and foreign aid. Yet the problems seem only to grow worse. And undoubtedly the reason is that for a great many people, even for the *imperatores* and *optimates*, their heart is not with the suffering and their needs but with themselves and their own ambitions. The money, the programs, are just a sop, not a cure.

In effect, then, most of the programs proposed seem little more than an attempt to buy peace of mind. The World Council of Churches, in a "radical" proposal, has suggested that each developed nation pledge one percent of its gross national product for the aid of the Third World. One percent! And that to be administered through an octopus-like bureaucracy with very sticky tentacles! Surely the thing that is needed is not more appropriations (5 percent?) but more dedication.

To return to our metaphor of Babylon and Zion, the Babylonian Jews did not appropriate a percentage of their money for the rebuilding of Jerusalem. On the contrary, only the individual Jews who responded to the call of God and who went out across the desert to Zion met the historic and spiritual challenge of the hour.

Conservative Christians, like political conservatives, have generally resisted massive bureaucratic, governmental, or even ecclesiastical programs as the wrong response to the needs of the day. And in this they are one with countless secular voices that denounce the growing anonymity of the individual, who becomes only a welfare number in an omnipotent and impersonal society. This resistance is always in the name of something better, something more personal. But where is that something better? In "False Presence in the Modern World,"[3] Jacques Ellul exposes the way in which the machinery of liberal and ecumenical Christendom simply echoes, parrot-like, the solutions of *tout le monde*, calling, in the name of Christ, for the world to be changed, by massive programs, in exactly the way envisaged by the secular bureaucrats, technologists—and revolutionaries.

But Jesus Christ did not send His followers into the world as parrots to echo the world's slogans and to approve the world's projects. He sent them as the salt of the earth, as the light of the world (MATTHEW 5:13–14). As Ellul writes, "The task is to mix with the world, rigorously refusing to be absorbed into it, preserving the specificity, the uniqueness, of the truth revealed in Christ, and of the new life which we receive from Him. The task is to carry forth the savor of salvation, of truth, of freedom, and of love which are in Christ, and never to allow oneself to be won over by the world with its strength, its splendor, its efficiency!"[4]

The task of rebuilding the waste places is a task that

[3] Jacques Ellul, *Fausse présence au monde moderne* (Paris: Les Bergers et les Mages, 1963).
[4] *Ibid.*, p. 42.

must be individual and cooperative. When the returning Jews reached Jerusalem, they had to be organized for effective labor and self-defense. But before this could take place, the vast majority had to return from Babylon, through the desert, under their own power—on foot. A decision had to be taken and a very substantial investment of personal energy and risk made before Nehemiah could have people worth organizing—it was no one percent investment, either.

The task facing the Christians and the churches today is to learn how *to be salt in the present age*. While the need to proclaim and to defend the Christian faith is never secondary, it is also never *solitary*. It is not enough for the Christians of our day merely to sound like salt: they must also taste and act like salt. Witnessing by words must be coordinated with lives lived and works done.

In a real sense, Christians today have unparalleled opportunities. Perhaps never before have the ruins been so evident, so thoroughly distributed throughout the world. And never before have the Christians living in the abundance of Babylon had such abundant means with which to rebuild them. What was the surplus wealth of the Jerusalem congregation in A.D. 40, which it shared with its widows and orphans? What was the wealth of Christians in Greece and Asia Minor in A.D. 55, many of them slaves, which they shared with St. Paul and with the mother church in Jerusalem? How many people had to get together to provide ship passage for Paul and his companions?

Today almost any individual Christian has the wherewithal to sacrifice some of the years of his life to witness to and work for others. Where a significant part of each college generation "drops out," through boredom and disgust, for one or more years, is there none to "fall out" for service? Where one home in eleven in America builds for itself a private swimming pool,[5] could not five or ten such families build a ghetto swimming pool? Of course there would be practical problems, but is that not the meat of the American middle class? If a doctor in general practice earns on the average of $31,000 per annum, is it not possible for five doctors in general practice to endow a sixth colleague for rural or urban slum work? Or is it better to wait until the tentacles of government financing have taken away every such possibility? Do we have too much leisure time, and are our hobbies, vacations, and pleasures becoming constantly more expensive? Does not the leisure time make it possible to do real work where it is needed, and the money make it possible to provide the necessary tools and supplies?

Nor should such an effort be limited to those who earn $31,000 a year and more. Is your income too small to enable you to pay one fifth of a doctor's salary? If so, have you then no time, no strength, no labor to put into the service of your neighbors, your community, the world?

This short study is primarily an examination of the class struggle, not a presentation of the solution to it. Yet if revolution is to be rejected, and reformation to be urged, it behooves us to say something, at least, about what this reformation must look like. It can take many forms, and be implemented in many ways. Much creative thought must be brought to bear on the planning and carrying out of its various phases. One thing is clear, however: those who wish to share in the work of reformation must turn their backs on Babylon. They must renounce the orientation of life about production for their own conspicuous consumption. Do not renounce production, like the hippies, to live off the surplus of the labors of others, but produce

[5] These and the following statistics are from *U.S. News and World Report*, February 16, 1970.

for a purpose: produce to meet the physical needs of a poor and wretched world. Man shall not live by bread *alone*, indeed. But it is hard to preach the Word of God to those who have *no* bread while you yourself eat cake!

What is needed, perhaps, is a kind of "social Gospel" in reverse. Advocates of the social Gospel of yesteryear, right up to WCC enthusiasts for "development" today, urged works of social action as the necessary preliminary to saving the poor and underprivileged. This is wrong. There is no "social minimum" necessary before a person can receive salvation in Christ—or did the good thief on the other cross (LUKE 23:40–43) have to be assured of decent living conditions before he could hear the promise of Jesus? But perhaps a "social Gospel" is the necessary preliminary for the salvation of the *rich!*

"How difficult it is for those that have riches to enter into the kingdom of God!" cried Jesus (LUKE 18:24). And today we all are rich in the West, with rare exceptions. Even Mr. Forman, demanding $500,000,000 in reparations, is a wealthy man by comparison with the majority of the world's population. His plane fare to San Antonio equalled the total average income of two or three Indians. A major cause of Negro discontent in the United States is the fact that they do not or cannot have the things they see *on their television sets!* In India, men are induced to undergo voluntary sterilization with the offer of a transistor radio; in the United States the most underprivileged have television. Of course, the economic problem is real, but even more serious is a cancer of the spirit, which affects rich and poor alike and which will prevent our reaching the solution for which we are violently grasping. In certain welfare offices it is seriously asked whether welfare recipients should be forbidden to own color television sets. (After all, if a poor old lady's children want to give her a little pleasure with a color T.V., surely it should be all right?) Without wishing to obscure the fact that serious economic problems and real hardship do exist even in America, it must be admitted that it takes some kind of Babylonian captivation of the spirit to buy a color T.V. for one's aged parent while leaving her to subsist on welfare payments!

Can the white man ever pay the black man enough reparations to compensate him for the history of slavery? And can the brazen agitator ever extort enough from the craven churchman *to be happy*? Or does the solution lie elsewhere? Is it possible that not only rich Americans and middle-class Americans, but even poor Americans are rich in the sense of LUKE 18? Certainly they are rich in the eyes of much of the world's population. Is it possible that the answer to materialistic cravings that are not being satisfied, and to the disgust that comes from those who are over-satisfied, lies in turning one's attentions to others? "For unto whomsoever much is given of him shall be much required" (LUKE 12:48).

The smug and self-satisfied of America and Europe are those who *like* Babylon, its cool waters, its hanging gardens. The rebels, the dropouts, are for the most part those who have *recognized* its selfishness and hypocrisy but have not *overcome* them. Selfishness poisons a man's spirit, and the only cure for selfishness is service. Hypocrisy seeks to deceive others about what we really are and the cure for hypocrisy is not frankness but a changed heart.

There is a way out of Babylon, even for the twentieth-century West. It involves renouncing the pursuits of gain and pleasure as the highest goals, to which secular men give themselves in theory and most Christians give themselves in practice; a social Gospel, not because the poor need to receive material things to be saved, but because the wealthy—and that includes most of us—need to learn to give them away to be saved. The Christians cannot *coerce* themselves or others to give up a portion of their wealth— that would be force, no different from revolutionary expropriation. But if they are persuaded that God is challenging them to a creative, caritative use of the vast wealth He has given them, they can choose to give it, and by their example even lead others in "a more perfect way." "No man can serve two masters: for either he will hate the one, and love the other, or else he will hold to the one, and despise the other. Ye cannot serve God and mammon" (MATTHEW 6:24).

10.

The Task of Reformation

SAYING No to revolution is necessary in order to be able to begin the work of reformation. By *reformation* we do not refer to a movement within Christendom, but to the influence that the Christian faith, believed, proclaimed, and practiced, should have on human society as a whole. Society is to be re-formed, given a new inner principle, according to the Word of God. This principle of reformation is *dynamic* but not violent, *organic* but not evolutionary.

Revolution is rejected as being the imposition by force of a new external form upon society with no real transformation of the lives of individuals or of the life of society. It should be clear that reformation by the Word of God does not mean the imposition upon society of certain principles derived from the Bible. That, like the revolution we reject, would involve a form of violence and it could change only the appearances of man's social systems but not their substance and spirit. The task of the Christian is to be a witness in the world, believing the Word of God, proclaiming it, and witnessing to it. His calling is to be salt or leaven, to transform the world by being active in it and yet distinct and different from it. Thus the Christian will be threatened by temptations from two sides: where there is power available to him the temptation will be to try to *conform* the world; where his power is weak, he will be tempted to conform *to* the world. He must preserve the distinctiveness and the clarity of his witness in the world, for otherwise he becomes salt that has lost its savor (MATTHEW 5:13). This is certainly a difficult task, one which can be fulfilled only by means of spiritual determination and discipline. It requires that the believer live in contact with the vital center of his faith, that he himself be *informed* by the Scriptures, and that he exercise himself in the life of discipleship. The process of transformation is never complete in an individual in this life, and if an individual is to have a part in the transformation of the world, he must be in constant transformation himself.

Christian Revolutionaries? What are we to say of those Christians who are sympathetic to revolution or even support it? First, we must remember St. Paul's warning that a servant is to be judged by his master, not by the other servants (ROMANS 14:4). In other words, if a Christian serves the cause of revolution and claims to be honoring God thereby, in the last analysis it is God who must judge him, not his fellow Christians. If such a Christian cannot be persuaded that violent revolution is not compatible with the teaching of Christ or the example of the early church, then it is the Master who must judge his conduct.

Genuine Christians who are genuine revolutionaries exist, but they are rare. Often resentment against ecclesiastical tyranny leads minority Christians to side with the party of revolution: thus the Communist party receives the support of some believing evangelicals in Italy, and likewise devout Roman Catholics may support Marxist goals in Northern Ireland. There are many more examples of support for revolution among those who are ostensibly Christian but who do not hold the historic Christian faith in any meaningful sense. When questioned about their faith, they often give evasive answers, refusing to confess that Jesus Christ is the Incarnate Son of God, virgin-born, crucified, risen, ascended, and coming again. Precisely because they do not worship Him, they see no need for either judgment or redemption, and, in Jacques Maritain's words, are "on their knees before the world," in effect worshipping this world and the power they think it has to redeem and renew itself.

Most, although not all, of the advocates of revolution within the churches are precisely such men. They no longer believe the Word of God and its message, and for this reason they cannot place much hope in its power to reform and transform men and society. But a man who does not believe in the transforming powers of God through His Word is no true Christian, whatever the position he may occupy.

We should be slow to criticize and condemn those Christians who, under great pressure, appear to compromise with non-Christian forces. No one with any understanding of the all-embracing terror of a truly totalitarian system can be indifferent to the plight of Christian leaders behind the Iron Curtain. It is easy for people living in bourgeois society to criticize them for lack of courage when they appear to compromise (or for lack of flexibility when they refuse to do so). Doubtless there is much hypocrisy, compromise, and even outright betrayal of Christ by churchmen in Communist countries—but we in the "free world" are often party to similar hypocrisy, compromise, and betrayal without even the threat of persecution to offer in extenuation.

The situation is thus different with churchmen and Christian political leaders in the West, who also bow to the powers and political ideologies that mock Christ and would eradicate His church by extending a friendly hand to anti-Christian rulers and according full recognition and reverence to their "Christian" puppets.[1] What shall we say of a professor of theology who sees in the attempts of a Communist nation to build a "new city" (incidentally, entirely without churches) a "sign of the Kingdom" without noticing who is its king? Or of an Anglican bishop who happily reported East German Communist acceptance of his best-known book as "atheistic propaganda," apparently not realizing that it *is* atheistic propaganda?[2] What about Rudolf Bultmann and his followers for whom Jesus Christ is alive only in the *kerygma,* that is, the proclamation of the Gospel?

The early church had a name for such people: *traditores.* It means "the handers-over," that is, those who placed the

[1] It is hard to give a fair and balanced judgment on the relationship between the World Council of Churches and other ecumenical and denominational groups on the one hand and the two church groupings behind the Iron Curtain on the other: the government-recognized church bodies which belong to the W.C.C. and other international associations, and the so-called "underground church" proclaimed by Pastor Richard Wurmbrand and discounted or denounced by others. I know from personal conversations that W.C.C. officials realize that many of the official church representatives from the Communist countries are stooges. One official of the W.C.C. from a Western country admitted to me at Uppsala in 1968, "We know that some of them are with the secret police, but we do not know which ones." I am persuaded that many of the W.C.C. leaders believe, in all good faith, that they must accept this state of affairs and pretend that it does not exist in order to be able to have any contact at all with the churches in Communist-dominated areas. They also feel that in time the governments concerned will be led to grant greater freedom to their churches. I am not persuaded that this policy is wise, and I believe that it involves intellectual dishonesty and compromise, but I cannot agree with what Pastor Wurmbrand seems to believe, namely that it means that all the officials and church leaders involved have betrayed the martyrs and sold out to world Communism. Their record is indeed questionable, but it does not help matters for the friends of the underground church to make sweeping statements of an unverifiable nature and then to brand anyone who questions them a Quisling and a traitor. An excellent and impartial orientation is given by the periodical *Religion in Communist Dominated Areas,* which should be in every public and church library (475 Riverside Drive, New York, N.Y. 10027).

heritage of the church into the hands of the persecutors. Becoming a *traditor* by handing over the Bible codices to the agents of the government was one step worse than being a *lapsus,* one who falls away. From *traditor* we derive our English word traitor. There are many such traitors in responsible positions in the church today, handing over the heritage of the church to those who seek to destroy it, and most of the "Christian" enthusiasts for revolution are such. There are of course some genuinely orthodox Christians who support revolution. The great majority, however, believes neither in Christ nor in changing society through changed men. Sometimes "Christian" adherents of revolution clearly admit their lack of faith in essential doctrines such as the Resurrection; sometimes they try to evade questions on such issues by saying that they are not the right questions to ask today, or by some similar subterfuge. In the present state of the churches, it seems impossible to dislodge such people—even those who plainly repudiate the faith—from their positions of honor and authority. (Even the late Bishop Pike, who was of course not a social revolutionary but a spiritual apostate, had to remove himself from his high office and ultimately from the Episcopal Church—the church preferred to leave him alone "to avoid scandal.") The believing elements of the various Christian churches at the least can label such *traditores* and dispute their right to speak in the name of Christ and of His church. Such a dispute and challenge may be a necessary preliminary to the positive work of reformation; a corrupt church cannot purify a corrupt society.

The reformation of a society by the Word of God does not involve the formal subjection of the society or the state to the Bible, which would, as we have said, simply be another kind of enforced conformation and not an inner reformation. Instead, it must involve the leavening action of convinced and dedicated Christians and groups, dispersed throughout society like yeast in a mass of dough. To this end the Christians must be *genuine*, as far as their own faith and life are concerned, and dynamic, moving out from the Christ-centered core to encounter and influence the society that surrounds them. This dynamism needs to have two dimensions, words and deeds—to use old-fashioned terminology, witnessing and good works. The reforming power and authority of the Word of God for individuals and for social relationships must be *proclaimed* and exhibited.

WITNESSING TO TRUTH

The Christian is called upon first of all to bear witness: to bear witness to the mighty acts of God, to His plan and to His purpose. The source of our knowledge of God's deeds, of His purposes, of His will for us is His Word. Bearing witness to the acts of God, then, involves testifying that the record of those acts is true and worthy of confidence. Thus the authority and trustworthiness of Scripture are of vital importance. In a world and an age where practical problems are so great, it may seem strange to demand first of all a theoretical approach, first of all a testimony to the truth and reliability of certain propositions, to the reliability of certain old documents. Would it not be more appropriate for Christians to pitch in with others of different faiths and of no faith at all in order to attempt to resolve the multiple problems which beset us, to feed the hungry, to heal the sick, to stop the wars? Do not actions speak louder than words? Actions do speak louder than words, but less clearly. Without actions words are unconvincing, but without words, actions may have no discernible meaning. Our world is in a *crisis of significance*; even feeding the hungry and healing the sick can become ambiguous actions if we do not know why we perform them. (Healing the sick—reducing infant mortality, for example—also increases population pressure, which may in turn promote war, and thus more misery and destruction than allowing sickness to keep populations down. In this case, the Christian knows *why* he should feed the hungry and heal the sick; not merely to alleviate present human suffering, but because God, in His Word, tells him to do so.) The Christian's necessary testimony to the truth of God's Word must be unashamed, tolerant, constant, and credible.

Unashamed. Christians are a minority group. Further, they are a minority group that is distinctive not by reason of appearance, social status, education, dress, or any other external factor, but by reason of what they believe. In the words of Christ Himself, Christians can be defined as "those we believe in Me through [the Apostles'] word" (JOHN 17:20). The Christians of today must face both their minority status and the fact that it depends on believing in Christ through the Apostles' word, that is, on believing the record of Scripture.

For the Christian living in a European country, or in North or South America, it may seem odd to talk of Christians as a minority group. What about the famous tradition of Christian civilization? Are we not "the Christian West"? Here two things must be noted: first, that the "Christian West" may very well once have had a kind of generally accepted Christian consensus, but that it has probably never had a majority of convinced Christians. Those who think of the Middle Ages as a wonderful "age of faith" may disabuse themselves of this notion by consulting a good history of medieval thought and life: can we speak of meaningful "faith" when many "Christians" did not even know the Lord's Prayer, the Ten Commandments, and the

Apostles' Creed?[3] The consensus, which accepted, in a general and superficial sort of way, the world-view of Catholic Christendom, did exist. Even though it was in many, perhaps most, cases hardly skin-deep, it gave a certain coloration to all of European society, and subsequently to American society. Today this consensus is rapidly vanishing, or has already vanished. The Christian who believes what Christ taught and who seeks to live by it is rapidly becoming a stranger even in those organizations called churches. Believing Christians are very much in the minority of the people in the world in the "Christian West," and even on the church membership rolls. As a minority, the Christians are called by God to give a firm, unashamed testimony in the teeth of unpopularity, opposition, and even persecution.

It is his distinctive *faith* which makes the Christian a Christian. Throughout the history of Christendom there has been a tendency to give the title "Christian" to all those who have any formal connection (usually by baptism) with a Christian church. According to this usage, a baptized adult who no longer believes or practices his Christianity (in other words, most of the people in "Christian" countries) should be called a "fallen-away Christian" or an "apostate," but not a non-Christian. The discussion over terminology is not very fruitful, but still we do well to reject this usage. It is evident that the baptized person without personal faith or conviction is not a Christian in any sense of the word that would have been acceptable to Christ or to His Apostles. A nonbeliever is a non-Christian. The expression "liberal Christian," applied to faith, is a contradiction in terms. A Christian may be "liberal" in his views on politics, law enforcement, etc., and still be a

[3] This melancholy picture is given by G. G. Coulton in *Five Centuries of Religion*, 4 vols. (Cambridge: Cambridge University Press, 1923–50).

Christian, although perhaps an inconsistent one. The person who is "liberal" in his theology, however, is not a Christian at all.*

The faith of the Christian in his Lord is a faith derived from a divine revelation, a revelation which comes to us *par excellence*, authoritatively, and worthy of our full trust, in the Holy Scripture, in the Bible. Without this revelation, no man can know God or His will. Unless the revelation in itself is trustworthy and reliable, no man can be confident that he can trust his knowledge of God which depends upon it. From the initial diabolical question that was posed to our first parents, the attempt to isolate man from God has always begun with the attempt to discredit God's words spoken to man: The serpent, "more subtil than any beast of the field which the Lord God had made," began his temptation of Eve, as we know, with the words, "Yea, hath God said . . . ?"

A firm confidence in the authority and trustworthiness of the Word of God has been characteristic of the whole Christian church, both before and after the Protestant Reformation, until our own century. Since the rise of Rationalism in the eighteenth century, the reliability, accuracy and authority of the Bible have been under fire from many quarters, originally from enemies of Christ, but now from those purporting to be His disciples. Only in our own century has the tendency to reject biblical authority come to be widespread. It is now quite common within the

---

* "Liberal" theological views, as opposed to the orthodoxy of the great ecumenical creeds and of the great confessions of faith (such as the *Confessio Augustana*, the Thirty-nine Articles, and the Westminster Confession), deny such biblical, evangelical, and catholic doctrines as the divinity of Christ, His physical Resurrection, His Virgin Birth and miracles, His substitutionary Atonement, and His Second Coming. Many members of the "ecumenical movement" (WCC), of course, reject the faith of the ecumenical creeds. That liberal Christianity is not Christianity at all is carefully shown by J. Gresham Machen in *Christianity and Liberalism* (New York: Macmillan, 1923; reissued, Grand Rapids: Eerdmans, 1960).

various Christian churches as well as outside them to look upon the Bible as at best a record of man's religious search, but not in any real sense inspired by God or authoritative. Needless to say, such an attitude rapidly destroys faith in Christ, for it is first and foremost the Scripture that speaks to us of Him. Far less needless to say, the major arguments against the accuracy and the reliability of Scripture have been around for a long, long time. A number of them go back to the second-century pagan philosopher Celsus; most others also have a long history. Only a few result from "modern scholarship"; more often than not, modern scholarship has cleared up long-standing problems. Unfortunately, much of what passes for "modern biblical scholarship," although it admits that the specific reasons for rejecting the reliability and accuracy of Old and New Testament passages have crumbled away, continues to reject them.[4]

Despite the widespread and confident attacks made everywhere on the trustworthiness of Scripture, the scholarly situation and the results of historical and archaeological research have never been more hospitable to a belief in biblical authority and inerrancy than they are today. It is not our purpose here to go into the attacks on the authority of Scripture and on the various possibilities of dealing with them; let it suffice for the moment to point out that there are many sound arguments in favor of biblical authority, and that modern archaeology has made them easier, not harder, to accept. The arguments in favor of it are not sufficient to *compel* belief, of course. Calvin, for example, took the position that confidence in the Scripture as the Word of God must come from the Scripture itself, made

[4] So Israeli scholar Yehezkel Kaufmann, speaking of the Old Testament, in *The Religion of Israel*, abridged translation by Moshe Greenberg (London: Allen and Unwin, 1961). Cf. the relevant essays in Carl F. H. Henry, ed., *Revelation and the Bible* (Grand Rapids: Baker, 1958), and Edward J. Young, *Thy Word Is Truth* (Grand Rapids: Eerdmans, 1957), esp. ch. 7.

plain and authenticated by the Holy Spirit, adding that once we have "received it in a manner worthy of its excellence, we shall then derive great assistance from things which before were not sufficient to establish the certainty of it in our minds."[5] This position seems valid today, for although the arguments in favor of biblical authority are by no means compelling, they are worthy of respect, and the arguments against it so often reveal faulty logic or facts, undisclosed presuppositions, or begin by assuming what they intend to prove, that no one who defends biblical authority need feel that he is sacrificing his reason to do so.

For example, attacks on the authority of the Bible usually begin with the so-called documentary hypothesis, which maintains that the first five or six books of the Bible were compiled from a miscellaneous collection of texts and fragments by a series of editors. One of the early adherents of this view, a man who later rejected it, Wilhelm Moeller, aptly characterizes the problem posed by this hypothesis for Christian faith as follows: "The more the authors of the Bible are seen not as writers but as collectors working with scissors and paste, who only arrange and organize various substrata which themselves also were produced by scissors-work, the more we will ask ourselves in vain how such a *mixtum compositum*, which is what the text of the Bible would be, could have the power it has to lead men's souls to God. This book would be as unique in its stupid origin as in its tremendous impact. Here we sense an unbearable contradiction."[6] But the documentary hypothesis, which has destroyed the faith of many and now, after so many years, is standard fare in most Protestant Sunday schools, as well as in the new Roman Catholic *Jerome*

---

[5] John Calvin, *Institutes of the Christian Religion*, Bk. I, Ch. 8:1.
[6] Wilhelm Moeller, *Wider den Bann der Quellenscheidung* (Gütersloh: Bertelsmann, 1912), pp. 219f. Cf. Umberto Cassuto, *The Documentary Hypothesis*, trans. Israel Abrahams (Jerusalem: Magnes Press, 1961).

Bible Commentary,[7] is the product of much fantastic speculation and is utterly undeserving of confidence. As the late Umberto Cassuto commented on the arguments behind it: "If you have no real ropes, but only figments of the imagination, even a thousand of them will not avail you to move the cart from its place. The sum of nought plus nought plus nought *ad infinitum* is only nought."[8] No adding of zeros ought to shake our confidence in the truth of the Book which authenticates itself as God's Word. It is good to know the arguments from which, as Calvin says, we can derive great assistance, but if we do not have the industry to study them, we should at least follow Moeller's advice as to the second-best recourse: "If scholarship attacks the Bible's vital power, it is the lesser error to limit ourselves to the following comment about its origin: 'We do not know and we never will know. We have experienced its power, and no so-called scholarship can deceive us about it.' "[9] We can therefore remain faithful to what St. Paul says: "I am not ashamed of the gospel of Christ, for it is the power of God unto salvation to every one that believeth" (ROMANS 1:16).

Tolerant. A firm confidence in the truthfulness of God's Word makes it possible for the Christian to be tolerant in witnessing to it. Much of the venom that Christians

---

[7] Two vols. (Englewood Cliffs, N.J.: Prentice-Hall, 1968), esp. Vol. I, Ch. 1.
[8] Cassuto, *op. cit.*, p. 101. Problems related to this and other widely held but quite wrong-headed theories about the reliability of biblical texts have been exposed by the noted Jewish scholar Cyrus Gordon, in "Higher Critics and Forbidden Fruit," *Christianity Today*, Nov. 23, 1959, pp. 131–134, and by many others, including: Kenneth A. Kitchen, *Ancient Orient and Old Testament* (London: Tyndale, 1966; Chicago: Inter-Varsity, 1967); Edwin Yamauchi, *Composition and Corroboration in Classical and Biblical Studies* (Philadelphia: Presbyterian and Reformed, 1966).
[9] Moeller, *op. cit.*, p. 220. Moeller points out that such resignation is not the best solution, but it is far better than to doubt the power of the Word of God on the authority of some very doubtful human scholarship.

often bring to theological and religious arguments stems from the fact that they are uncertain of their own convictions. Of course, there is a place where anger at those who deny the truthfulness of God's Word is hard to avoid; this is especially the case when the deniers pretend to be His spokesmen. It will never be easy for a believing Christian to be tolerant of bishops, clergy, and theology professors who pretend to be speaking for God but who actually repeat the devil's sly question, "Yea, hath God said . . . ?" A confidence in God's Word, far from making the believing Christian intolerant of those who do not believe, should make it possible for him to bear a confident, tolerant witness, "speaking the truth in love" (EPHESIANS 4:15), pleading and persuading men as Christ's ambassadors, as St. Paul says (II CORINTHIANS 5:20). The confidence he has in God's Word should keep him from ever trying to compel others and from ever failing to recognize that it is the Holy Spirit who gives the final conviction, not the force or intensity of our arguments.

An awareness of the fundamental fact that it is God Himself who must perform the miracle of conversion, and that we are to bear witness but not to belabor our neighbors, should make it possible for a Christian's witness to be fully faithful to Christ and at the same time gentle and tolerant towards those who will not accept it. This principle of tolerance becomes possible *because of* a full and unashamed confidence in the truthfulness of Holy Scripture and its revelation as the Word of God. It makes a significant demand upon our witnessing: it demands that it be constant, precisely because it never compels.

Constant and Persistent. The very fact that the Christian must renounce any tactics of compulsion in attempting to win others to Christ makes it all the more important that his witness to Him be constant. It must never become a one-shot affair after the manner of the prayer of the farmer who, growing tired of kneeling every night on the cold floor of his unheated bedroom, wrote out his petitions and tacked them on the wall over his bed. After that he would kneel just long enough to nod to the written prayers on the wall and to say, "Lord, them's my sentiments," before jumping into bed. Prayer must be constantly renewed, and in the same manner witness must be constant. As Karl Heim writes of the Christian's life as a witness, any encounter "may be the occasion which will bring about the great all-transforming discovery in a man's life. Because this possibility is always present, even though I never have control over it, it must be the most intense desire of every believer that he may act and speak and write in such a way that his whole existence, both active and passive, may be for those around him the 'occasion' which brings about the great event, the discovery of the space of God, even for those from whom this space was hitherto concealed."[10] The everyday Christian, no less than St. Peter and St. John before the Jewish Sanhedrin, should be one who speaks out of an inner necessity. They said, "We cannot but speak of what we have seen and heard" (ACTS 4:20). It is not enough merely to be labeled a Christian, merely to "fly the flag," although that is important; it is necessary also to be constant in bearing an unmistakable witness to the One who is the way, the truth, and the life.

Living the Truth. As Dr. Francis A. Schaeffer points out in *The God Who Is There*,[11] truth comes before conversion:

[10] Karl Heim, *Christian Faith and Natural Science*, trans. H. Norton Smith (New York: Harper, 1953; Harper Torchbooks, 1957), pp. 246f. By the expression "the space of God," Heim refers to an awareness of the reality of the personal God of the Bible.
[11] London: Hodder, and Chicago: Inter-Varsity, 1968. Cf. esp. pp. 143ff.

unless a man realizes the existence of real truth—whether or not he has an epistemological explanation of it is less important—he cannot understand or accept the claims of Christ. Truth also stands after conversion: if what we believe and confess is true, we must exhibit its truth and live it out in our lives. Otherwise God remains true, but we are false Christians and very unconvincing witnesses. Living out in our lives the truth to which we give formal allegiance is crucial in the task of the reformation of individuals and of society according to the Word of God. It means attesting and manifesting the reconciling and the renewing power of God's Word in His world.

RECONCILING POWER: THE MESSAGE AND ITS CONSEQUENCES

Are all men created equal? This idea, long preached in America as self-evident, no longer seems either self-evident or necessarily true. The Black Power movement in America demonstrates the fact that the mere removal of external, legal barriers to an individual's economic and social advancement does not necessarily mean that he will advance. There have been relatively few attempts to evaluate racial differences objectively; usually the superiority of one race or the equality of all races has been dogmatically asserted. At the present time, no really convincing evidence for or against the equality of races has been presented. It seems unlikely, in view of the variety seen among different animal races, that there are no significant differences in ability among the races of man. This in itself is not so important, however, because it is quite evident that there are significant differences among individual human beings of the same race. Whether they are caused by environment or by heredity may be disputed, but in fact they amount to an inequality, and often a very severe one, in the contest of life. In earlier chapters the various class struggles arising out of these inequalities have been discussed. Taken together, they are all exploited by the diabolos in his role as divider. Dividing men from each other, he convinces us that our group incarnates Good while another incarnates Evil, and thus tricks us into committing evil actions against our "evil" neighbors and ignoring the evil that is within us. Thus he cuts us off from God as well.

There is no empirical proof that all men are equal, nor is there likely to be. There are many different standards by which we can and do evaluate each other, our own and other races, and each of them may "justify" our contempt for other men, or for another race, culture, or class. There is only one very important sense in which all human beings are equal: they are all equal before God. All men are born, having had no voice in the matter, and all men die, having no way to avoid it. Apart from Christ, they are all equally lost; with Christ, they are children of one Father, and all human barriers of race and class become meaningless.

Equality apart from Christ is a real, if dreadful, thing. The Christian should have no hesitancy in pointing out this awful equality. Non-Christian thinkers from the great Greek tragic poets of the fifth century before Christ to the existentialist philosophers and novelists of our own day, although not recognizing or admitting *why* man is lost, universally see him as an abandoned waif in a hostile universe, the spoil of blind powers that condemn him to an absurd existence and to a meaningless and futile death. The Christian can agree with this, and at the same time he can point with greater insistency and enthusiasm to the opportunity of a positive, joyous equality as children of God. The message of God's Word, then, is that "there is neither

Jew nor Greek, there is neither slave nor free, there is neither male nor female; for you are all one in Christ Jesus" (GALATIANS 3:28; cf. COLOSSIANS 3:11).

The fact of this fundamental equality must be lived if Christians are to be credible witnesses and are to aspire to a reformation of the individual and of his society. It does not necessarily mean legislation to abolish discrimination and racial or class distinctions; such legislation was neither demanded nor enacted by the early Christians. Slaves often remained slaves, and masters masters. But it means that both slave and master are to fulfill their duties and mutual obligations as brothers, as fellow servants of Christ (EPHE-SIANS 6:5–9). This does not exclude social change; in fact, it rather speaks for it, for a brother will find it hard to impose onerous and unequal service upon his brother. But it provides something more important than social change. A change in the hearts of men can render an inegalitarian social structure livable, while human coldness and indifference can make a hell out of a situation of perfect equality (as Jean-Paul Sartre so cruelly illustrated in No Exit).

What does this mean in the specific social situation of our day? It means, first of all, that Christians must become aware that their primary identification is with Christ, and through Him, with their fellow Christians. It is of primary importance to be a Christian and only of secondary importance that one is a banker or a factory worker, a manager or a housemaid, a Caucasian or a Negro. By developing a consciousness of this primary identification, the Christian will discover a true brotherhood with those who are richer than he, poorer than he, older, younger, and of different racial heritage, educational background, and occupational skills.

It may be objected that such a Christian brotherhood, even if it were to be fully realized, would not change the situation for the majority of society's people, who are not believing Christians. It would prove the elimination of human divisions to be possible within a limited religious fellowship, but it would thereby accentuate the divisions between those *in* the fellowship and those *outside* it. To this objection, two answers may be made.

First, the example of interracial, interclass, interage fellowship is contagious. As St. Paul said, "A little yeast leavens the whole lump" (GALATIANS 5:9). We should not underestimate the effect of a good example in influencing society. Christ himself gives the second reason: He gave His followers the command to love each other, and told them that by their obedience to it, men would recognize them as *His* disciples (JOHN 13:35). The example of a living Christian brotherhood spanning class, racial, age, and other distinctions would thus be a vital way to witness to Him. And this brings us to the significance of this second answer. The Christian may help his non-Christian fellow citizens by deed and example, because the teachings of Christ do in effect bring benefits to those who do not espouse them, but the Christian can never pretend to offer a full solution to man's problems apart from Christ.

If Christian groups, by obedience to the Word of God, resolve social problems in a way in which others, who do not believe in the Christian faith, cannot be expected to follow, that is as it should be. Christians are called upon to heal the divisions of mankind *within* their community of faith precisely so that others may come to share that faith. A Christian reformation of society by persuasion and example would bring more happiness and less misery to non-Christians than either the violent revolution or the authoritarian repression of which we have spoken, but that is not the principal reason for the Christian to seek it. His principal reason must be obedience to the will and purpose of God, as made known to him through His Word. A central part of God's purpose is the spread of the Gospel; living out His teachings in the reformation of society will also spread the Gospel. As Karl Heim said, it must be the desire of every believer to *act*, to speak, and to write in such a way that others will come to know and to believe in his Lord. Thus fellowship must be acted out as well as proclaimed.

Practical Applications. The practical impact of the reconciling power of the Word of God will be felt if Christians begin, openly and unashamedly, to practice *Christian discrimination*, in the sense that St. Paul meant when he wrote, "Do good unto all men, but especially unto them who are of the household of the faith" (GALATIANS 6:10). The Christian has an obligation towards all, but a special obligation towards those who are bound up with him in the Body of Christ. Unfortunately, generalized love, like generalized kindness, is very difficult to achieve. It must begin with individuals, and *a fortiori* with the individuals to whom one stands in a close relationship through loyalty to the same Lord. This can take place, of course, only if Christians become accustomed openly to confess their faith —and not in saying something like, "I belong to such and such church," but rather "I am a believer in the Christ of the Scriptures and of the historic creeds."

Having once established the existence of membership in the community of faith, the Christian as a practical step must seek to express this community across racial, social, economic, and educational lines. This can be encouraged by taking some simple steps of self-discipline, namely, by seeking out those who belong to other classes (races, age groups, etc.). More important than this, however, is the cultivation of his own inner conviction that the central and most crucial identity comes from Christ and not from class. In order to obtain this conviction, preaching, teaching, personal study and meditation will all have to concentrate considerable attention on the Christian's relationship to his Lord and membership in His mystical Body, the Church.

Most current preaching falls into one of three main categories: they may loosely be called the evangelistic, the dogmatic, and the edifying types of sermon. An edifying sermon may seek to confront the listeners with a specific problem or situation and to encourage them to respond in a certain way; often no attempt is made to explain *why* a "Christian" response is indicated, nor to ascertain whether in fact the listeners are committed to follow Christ at all. The dogmatic sermon teaches certain aspects of Christian doctrine, again often without engaging the listener or making him examine his own relationship to Christ. Only the evangelistic type of sermon, as a rule, seeks to make the listener ask himself about his personal relationship to Christ. Unfortunately, evangelistic sermons often lead only to the point of personal conversion, but not beyond, into practical Christian living. The deepening of the relationship and, above all, the increasing of personal awareness of what it can and should mean are not usually sought in such a sermon. All three types may fail to help the person who is honestly committed to Christ to grow in his understanding and implementation of what this relationship means. What is necessary, then, is to deepen the believer's sense of his distinctive identity as a Christian and to make it stronger and more profound. If this is done, reconciliation between Christians of different classes and backgrounds will not be difficult. With this as a solid foundation, the Christian brotherhood can work for the reformation of society and the conversion of individuals.

11.

Affirmations

THE class struggle in its various forms is the devil's program. It sets men against each other, and it encourages them in the delusion that evil can be destroyed by destroying one's opponents in a given struggle. In biblical terms, it encourages us to behold the mote in another's eye and to ignore the beam in our own—a sure recipe for blindness. To reject the mentality of the class struggle in all its manifestations, to refuse to play this particular game of the devil's, is especially important at this juncture in history. Whether or not we agree with the late existentialist philosopher Karl Jaspers (d. 1969) that certain revolutionary governments are entirely capable of destroying the human spirit,[1] we have to admit that the danger of total tyranny has never been so great, and that the class struggle is sure to promote it.

If we pray, "Thy will be done on earth," we must also

---

[1] In *Die Atombombe und die Zukunft der Menschheit* (Munich, 1958), Jaspers argues that Communist tyranny is so deadening to all that is human that it would be better to fight an atomic war and risk the annihilation of the human race than to submit to such dehumanizing domination. In other words, for this philosopher, to whom freedom was an essential requirement for *human* existence, the slogan was, "Better dead than Red!" The courage it takes for a man who does not believe in eternal life to say this should put many weak-spirited Christians to shame.

be prepared to do what we can to obey and to accomplish God's will, even admitting that there is much that only He Himself can bring to pass. A first step is to reject and to resist those things which go against His will; specifically, to oppose the destructive madness of the struggle for dominance—the class struggle—in all its contemporary manifestations. Of course, this is not sufficient; merely to oppose those things which oppose God's will is not to fulfill it. We need not apologize for having been negative. In a fallen world, any movement which seeks the good must spend a great deal of its time fighting evil—even the utopian revolutionaries devote much of their energy to smashing the existing order. However, precisely because we have claimed that their plans are destructive and will lead to tyranny and to dehumanization, we must offer affirmative alternatives. If God's will is not to be fulfilled by destructive class struggle, how is it to be accomplished?

At this point, when we begin to speak positively about God's will, the Christian quickly parts company with the secular humanist. The Christian knows, as Martin Luther so emphatically said, that "God will not be seen, known, or comprehended except through His Word alone. Whatever, therefore, one undertakes for salvation apart from the Word is in vain."[2] The secular humanist or philanthropist ought to agree with the biblical Christian that general human welfare will not be served by the ethics of class struggle or by the survival of the fittest, but—apart from conversion—he will not follow the Christian in seeking it in obedience to the Word of God. Here the Christian must take the consequence of the situation in which he finds himself: united by faith, by what is called the new birth, with a fellowship of believers who have heard and responded to God's voice, and united by blood, society, and human

[2] Luther, *Werke*, Weimarer Ausgabe, XLVIII, 148.

heritage to all his fellow human beings who have not yet discerned God's voice in the same way. He is faced with the twofold task of serving Him and helping them.

FIDELITY

This is not an easy task, and that should not surprise us. Obedience to God can hardly be easy in a world in rebellion against Him. In some ways, it seems simpler and safer to flee the world and its perils, but we know that this is not the calling of the majority of Christians, whose job it is to serve the world in which God has placed them. A fundamental principle, one which has been largely abandoned by many ecumenical and "social Gospel" enthusiasts, is that one serves the world best by remaining faithful to God. One does not serve it by accommodation to its natural inclinations. To do so will reduce friction—but is it good for a fallen world to be tranquil? No one expects or wants a doctor to become infected with the flu in order to help his flu patients. Sometimes contamination and contagion cannot be avoided. Many doctors are infected by their patients, and some die. But no doctor who catches the same disease as his patients have thinks that thereby he has done them a service: he hopes that his medical knowledge will enable him to cure himself as well.

In the spiritual realm, the Christian is called upon to be a faithful witness. He can help a confused and erring world most by remaining as faithful as possible to the light he has seen, not by extinguishing it. There may well have been a time when Christians were too exclusive, self-confident, and self-righteous. Today their danger lies in sharing the confusion of the world apart from God and His revelation, not in holding too narrowly to them. Army chaplains are told that they can serve soldiers of other faiths better by

remaining true to their own, rather than by trying to imagine what they might say if they were someone else; likewise,
the Christian should recognize that he can best help the
unbelieving world by being loyal, faithful, and consistent
to what he believes. The mere example of a principled,
inner-directed man is worth something today! The Christian knows that the world was made by God and that man
was created for fellowship with Him. However disagreeable
undiluted Christian teaching, Christian faith, and Christian morals may appear to those who do not accept them,
they remain valuable only if unadulterated. Christians still
have much to learn in the area of practical tolerance; even
St. Paul, who never minced words to spare people's feelings,
saw the necessity of "speaking the truth *in love*" (EPHESIANS
4:15). Still, it must be speaking the *truth*, for otherwise it
is pure wishful thinking, and no help to anyone. The Christian thus must keep coming back, with constantly increased
confidence to *all* the teachings of God's Word, to the hard
ones ("If any will not work, let him not eat," II THESSA-
LONIANS 3:10) as well as the mild ones ("Do good to all
men," GALATIANS 6:10). Only as he bears witness to God's
trustworthiness in all His words and works can the Christian's faith appear credible or even plausible to anyone who
stands outside it.

This fidelity should result in self-identification, in a conscious admission that it is *as a Christian* that one is under-
taking political and social responsibilities. There is no Christian system of government or economics as such, but
Christian voters, politicians, workers, and industrial managers
must all seek to act in accordance with God's will in the
exercise of their this-worldly obligations. Earthly responsibilities should be consciously and openly undertaken *before
God*, both in obedience to Him and as a means of bearing
witness to the world. Only in this way can Christians be,

in Jesus' words, "the salt of the earth" (MATTHEW 5:13), pungent, bitter perhaps, but indispensable. Nothing is more dispensable than salt which has lost its ability to season! Often a Christian feels quite hesitant to speak or even to vote *as a Christian* on an issue which also affects his non-Christian fellow citizens. Nevertheless, this is the only way to preserve one's Christian and human integrity. The very tolerance which accords to others the freedom to obey their own convictions requires that I obey and profess my own. A belligerent Puritan is disagreeable, but a lukewarm one is disgusting. During imperial Rome's persecution of the church, Christians did not water down either Christ's claims to exclusive authority or the stern demands of Christian ethics, but they did maintain that despite society's hostility to them, their influence was beneficial to it. Their prayers, their seriousness, and their industry all helped preserve, for a time at least, the declining Empire. Even anti-Christian propagandists in the contemporary Soviet Union have sometimes been forced to concede the contribution which Soviet Christians make to the general welfare, simply because their Christian conscience leads them to fulfill their this-worldly obligations to society as before God. Thus the despised Christians are often more conscientious than those who are motivated only by "socialist morality." In a day when hardly anyone seems ashamed to say that he is living for himself, for his own comfort, and his own pleasure, it would be laughable—and foolish—for Christians to be ashamed to admit that they are living for God!

DISCERNMENT

St. John speaks of the need to "test the spirits" (1 JOHN 4:1), a need which existed even within the earliest Christian community, the primitive church. It should not surprise us, nineteen hundred years removed in time from those early congregations, that we too must exercise a like discretion. The Apostle who gave us the phrase, "God is love" (I JOHN 4:8), was the same man who said that a false teacher—one who refused to acknowledge the Incarnation of Christ—should not be welcomed into a Christian's house, or even given a Christian greeting (II JOHN 10). Naturally St. John refers to *pretended Christians*, not to admitted non-Christians. For a believing Christian, it is quite natural to associate and cooperate with forthright non-Christians, whereas it is difficult to preserve even outward standards of tact with those who claim to be Christians while denying and often ridiculing fundamental Christian doctrines. It would be considered a gross breach of good taste, and rightly so, to address a meeting of Jews and ridicule Moses; with "liberal" Jews one might get away with it, but even then it would be discourteous, and among reverent Jews it would surely provoke a hostile response, perhaps even more hostile if the mocker were himself a Jew than if he were a Gentile. It is both natural and necessary for the believing Christian to react against the type of turncoat "Christian" who profanes Christ and dishonors His teachings.

Unfortunately, as C. S. Lewis pointed out several years ago, the word "Christian," like the word "gentleman," has lost its original definite meaning for many people. Thus to say of someone, "he is not a Christian," is seemingly to accuse him of being a scoundrel. Therefore it would be good if we could restrict the use of the word "Christian" to those persons, organizations, doctrines, etc., that really are in harmony with the historic ecumenical creeds and with fundamental biblical principles. Persons who hold and teach antibiblical and non-Christian doctrines should plainly be called non-Christians. One might be tempted to call them apostate Christians, but that would imply that they once held the faith and have subsequently turned away from it. The Germans* seem to have found a solution, inasmuch as many of them prefer to refer to themselves as "theologians" rather than as Christians. In their eyes "theology" —by which they mean a particular kind of academic tradition—is a far better guide to faith and practice than are the words of Christ and His Apostles, an attitude which may merit the title "theological" but which certainly is not Christian.

Whatever we want to call those teachers, preachers, and administrators who no longer respect the authority of Scripture or seek to conform their teaching and lives to it, it is clear that it would be better to risk occasional hurt feelings and even to have to apologize from time to time than to spread perpetual confusion among Christians and non-Christians alike by conceding the name Christian to everyone who does not declare himself to be something else.

Discernment, then, must take a high priority in our attempts to achieve a consistent life of Christian witness and work in the world. It is becoming increasingly necessary to refuse the name of Christian to members and leaders of one's own confession or denomination. Fortunately many of the apostate theologians and church leaders make their defection reasonably clear by the stand they take, and a number of them have clearly abandoned Christian distinctives, albeit retaining the name Christian. As the label "Christian" ceases to bring them social acceptability, many modern church leaders set less and less store by it; perhaps some of them will drop it altogether and leave it to those who really are committed to faith in Christ according to the Apostles' testimony. For the moment, however, it is necessary to examine the source of all "Christian" pro-

* Or at least the most celebrated theologians of Germany.

nouncements and contributions to current discussion, and
to see whether they are consistent with the Scriptural standards. This is an important reason why individual Christians
should know the Bible well, for otherwise they have no
defense against being duped by plausible-sounding theological and ecclesiastical confidence men.

Discernment is equally necessary in another area: the
recognition of brethren with whom one can make common
cause in other denominations and communions. The differences that divide orthodox Roman Catholics from orthodox
Lutherans and Calvinists, for example, are not *insigni-
ficant*, but they are *far less significant* than those within
Catholicism between the orthodox and the various kinds
of radicals. The same holds true of the Protestant communions. An awareness of this is growing on many sides, and
we now see signs of practical cooperation and fellowship
between believing Catholics and Protestants—just as radical Protestants and liberal Catholics happily help each other
tear down their institutions and undermine their faith.
Christians of various backgrounds and affiliations should
be constantly on the lookout for spiritual allies in other
Christian bodies. Just as persecution tends to make the
different parties draw together, so widespread disloyalty to
Christ and His teaching *within* the individual churches is
a stimulus to look for those who are loyal to fundamental
Christian doctrines and principles beyond one's own ecclesiastical borders.

RECONCILIATION

Once the principles of *fidelity* and of *discernment* have
been recognized and put into practice, Christians can pur-
sue their task of fulfilling God's will for human society,
assured of moving in the right direction and with the right

company. Un-Christian motives and means, such as "the survival of the fittest" and "class struggle," will be abandoned, and biblical motives and means will come into the foreground. At this point the Christian alternative to revolution must actually appear; if it does not, all that has been said in criticism of violent revolution and rebellion may look like nothing more than a rationalization for selfish conservatism (that is, the conservation, at all costs, of what I possess). As Christ Himself said, "You will know them by their fruits" (MATTHEW 7:16). Human society is in drastic need of really *fruitful* reforms. The violent struggles which we have discussed, and which are perfectly capable of tearing society apart, cannot be suppressed indefinitely. They must be healed and their causes dealt with. This can only be done under the sign of reconciliation. We have rejected all attempts to purge society of evil by eliminating allegedly evil classes, and said that the work of reform must begin in the lives of individuals. Well then, it must begin; if no practical fruits appear, how can this supposedly Christian answer to the diabolical temptation of class struggle be an answer at all?

Reconciliation must take place in two dimensions: vertical (man to God) and horizontal (man to man). The vertical (conversion) is *essential*, but the horizontal is not optional. Witnessing to the truth of Christ's teaching by expressing it in verbal form (evangelism, apologetics) is necessary if it is to be believed; practicing His teaching is necessary if *we* are to be believed. This means reconciliation and reformation in social problems. Through the centuries, in various ways, Christians have protested that human society cannot be *legislated* into the Kingdom of God, nor even into its secular perversions, the utopian monarchy of Marx or of the Great Society. Individual humans must be persuaded, won, changed as individuals. Very well, then;

the analysis seems sound. But a problem remains. Someone once said, "Christianity has not been tried and found wanting; it has been found hard and not tried." There are exceptions to this "not tried" in the realm of faith: people have tried Christian belief. There have been exceptions in the practical realm too: the history of the church does boast many outstanding examples of men and women who have put Christ's social principles into practice on an individual, day-to-day basis. The trouble is that they *stand out*, that is, they are rare.

The Christian may rightly protest that the government cannot compel white men to love black men, or vice versa. That is true, but the love of Christ can and will so compel them, if an opportunity is sought. So mass marches, "freedom rides," bussing, and civil riots are wrong, and a one-to-one relationship is right. Fair enough, but then, let there be some such relationships!

Prior to the present era of civil rights legislation, practical opportunities for white-black contacts were limited; now they are much more numerous. But the antirevolutionary Christian, to be credible, must seek them out. We reject "artificial" and forced mixing; very well, let us build some practical, personal alternatives. This must not be limited to racial contacts. The Christian should cultivate contacts and fellowship between classes, professions, occupational groups, and age groups. Naturally such contacts will have to remain somewhat limited; naturally men and women of a particular age, race, and class will still tend to stick together. Efforts may remain "token" ones, but the much-derided "tokenism" is not necessarily wrong. Individual Christians *ought* to be tokens (from Anglo-Saxon *tacen*, a visible sign) of God's reconciling purpose by their mere presence in places where they would not otherwise be expected to be. Of course, fidelity to the Gospel is crucial:

they must be present *as Christians, as witnesses* to Christ. But they must *be present*. This means that individual Christians and Christian congregations must be alert to every opportunity for a symbolic ("token") breaking of class, race, and age barriers. Such tokens become a pledge of full reconciliation in the Kingdom of God. Of course this will not be easy; of course there will be friction and embarrassment. Nevertheless, God calls us to it: individual penetration and participation are a Christian alternative to government coercion and coordination, but only if we exercise it.

Churches do not want to submit to extortion. Nor should they; to do so would be foolish as well as humiliating. "Millions for reconciliation, but not one penny for extortion!" Very well, then let some of the millions actually be *spent* for reconciliation. We reject mass government programs which seem to reward idleness and to penalize personal industry and self-help. "If any will not work, let him not eat." But what about the people "who do not know their right hand from their left" (JONAH 4:11)? Can they find work? No, but (except for rare exceptions) they can be taught, they can be led out (educate: from Latin *e-duco*, lead out) of their crippling ignorance and lethargy. Paul's strict economic justice imposes an obligation to teach. You cannot legislate learning or enterprise, but you can stimulate them. This is the task of individuals and of voluntary associations; it is a task in which the church excelled in its early days, even under persecution, and in mission lands, even under adverse conditions. It is a task which must be taken up again, in our "Christian" or post-Christian West, not just to avoid or to bypass mass government intervention, but because God wills it. "Let your light so shine before men," Jesus told His followers, "that they may see your good works and give glory to your Father who is in heaven" (MATTHEW 5:16). But what churches today are serious about fulfilling this expression of God's will? "Liberal" churches ignore it, preferring lobbying in Washington and social disruption nearer to home; evangelical ones, which ought to know better, have also laid it aside, to defend "the faith," "the truth of the Gospel." But—as St. James says, *in* the New Testament, and not in a comment *on* the New Testament—"As the body apart from the spirit is dead, so faith apart from works is dead" (JAMES 2:26).

The answer to the error of the social Gospel—that Christianity consists in promoting social betterment—does not lie in opposing social change, but in showing that changed men can change society. The true alternative to revolution with its mass murder is not repression, to convert society into a mass prison. It is the alternative of individual change, of reformation. This is the secret of the Christian answer to Marx and to other secularist Utopias: the Kingdom of God is not an external regime, it is an inward regeneration, God's rule in the hearts of individuals. It will not be fulfilled until the return of Christ, but it can be approached; indeed, it must be approached, for how can one presume to say that God's will rules in our hearts if our hands do nothing to fulfill it in the world in which He has placed us?

No individual, no congregation, no church can do everything—but then *neither can any government*. Because we cannot do everything, because there is so much to do, there is all the more reason to do something. No Christian can live a life of perfect self-discipline, nor is he expected to do so. Nowhere does Jesus command, as a general rule, that the appetites of the body are to be ruthlessly suppressed. With the exception of sexual infidelity, there are few indulgences which are rigorously prohibited in the Bible. The principle, "Make no provision for the flesh, to gratify its desires" (ROMANS 13:14), does not mean that no fleshly appetites are to be fulfilled, for that would mean death.

CONCENTRATION AND METHOD

To say that what is necessary for the reformation of society cannot and should not be done by government decree or by revolutionary action does not mean that it must be done spontaneously, without reflection and without method. What we have tried to do in these pages is a necessary first step: to shake the Christian community out of its hypnotic fascination with the delusion that the structures of bigness are the secret of renewal, and to free it from the sway of turncoat leaders who would place the church of Christ in the service of the devil's chaos. This first step may be likened to draining a marshy construction site; if it is not done, you cannot build anything of value, but drainage is not building. The work of drainage must be followed by actual construction.

We want to avoid building modern equivalents of the Pyramids, which squandered the lives and strength of tens of thousands to make a final resting place for the corpse of a single man. We want instead to build houses for habitation, in which individuals and families can live and grow. But even the construction of single houses, though tiny by comparison with the Pyramids, requires planning and method.

The renunciation of pyramid-building means that Christians will not pretend to have some kind of divine authority to tell the world's non-Christian majority what social, political, and economic structures it ought to establish. The determination to build houses means that we must develop, as individuals, congregations, and churches, practical, person-to-person methods of putting biblical principles into action. When people expect that every important change must come by government *fiat*, their individual contributions consist largely in arguing about what the government should do (or, if conservatives, about what it should not do). The Christian principle is that it is through our individual contributions that God builds; as St. Paul writes, "You are the building God is constructing" (I CORINTHIANS 3:9). The Gospel makes it clear that, contrary to popular assumptions, God builds through people who fulfill His will, not through "revolutionary social change." This fulfillment must take on practical, detailed dimensions. No individual, no congregation can do everything, but each can do something. The challenge to individuals who reject the statist solutions of the mass-thinkers and call for a Christian alternative is to work out that alternative, not for the whole world, but for themselves and in their particular life-situations.

We have likened the extortioners' claims being made on churches today to highway robbery. To the traditional highwayman's demand, "Your money or your life!" today's Christians must find their own ways to respond, "Not my money—my life!"

Index

HAROLD O. J. BROWN has also served in 1970–1971 as Visiting Lecturer in Theology, Union Biblical Seminary, Yeotmal, Maharashtra, India. He was called and served briefly as Professor of Church History at the new Free Evangelical Theological Academy of Basel, Switzerland (1970–1971), but resigned this post together with the position of Theological Secretary of the I.F.E.S. effective October 1, 1971, to join the staff of *Christianity Today*. During the Fall Quarter of 1971 he is Visiting Professor of Theology at Trinity Evangelical Divinity School in Deerfield, Illinois. The Browns have one daughter, Cynthia Anne. After January 1, they will make their home in the Washington, D.C., area.